....

A CIVILIZED TRAVELLER'S
GUIDE TO TURIN

....

A CIVILIZED TRAVELLER'S
GUIDE TO

TURIN

by Eugenia Bell

THE LITTLE BOOKROOM
NEW YORK

Book Design by Louise Fili Ltd

Printed in the U.S.A. by Worzalla

Cover image: Gran Madre and Monte dei Cappuccini.
Courtesy of Turismo Torino.

Library of Congress Cataloging-in-Publication Data

Bell, Eugenia.
A civilized traveller's guide to Turin / Eugenia F. Bell.
p. cm.
ISBN 1-892145-35-9 (alk. paper)
1. Turin (Italy)—Guidebooks. I. Title.
DG975.T94B37 2006
914.5'120493—dc22
2005023547

Published by The Little Bookroom
1755 Broadway, Fifth floor
New York, NY 10019
(212) 293-1643
(212) 333-5374 fax
editorial@littlebookroom.com
www.littlebookroom.com

Distributed the UK by Macmillan Distribution Ltd.

To EMA for whom Turin was a given
and to MAW for whom Turin was a gift.

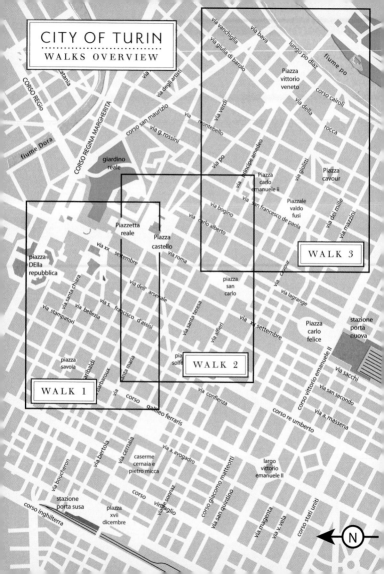

CITY OF TURIN
WALKS OVERVIEW

CORSO REGIO

via catania

via

via degli antisti

CORSO REGINA MARGHERITA

corso san maurizio

via g. rossini

via montebello

via verdi

via vanchiglia

via bava

via giulia di barolo

lungo po diaz

fiume po

Piazza vittorio veneto

corso cairoli

via della rocca

fiume Dora

giardino reale

via principe amedeo

via po

Piazza carlo emanuele ii

via san francesco de paola

via giolitti

Piazza cavour

Piazzale valdo fusi

via del mille

via mazzini

piazza DElla repubblica

Piazzetta reale

Piazza castello

via xx settembre

via s. francisco d'assisi

via dell' arsenale

via roma

via santa chiara

via bellezia

via stampatori

via bogino

via carlo alberto

piazza san carlo

via santa teresa

via alfieri

via xx settembre

via cavour

via lagrange

Piazza carlo felice

stazione porta nuova

via sacchi

WALK 3

WALK 2

WALK 1

piazza savoia

via garibaldi

via barbaroux

via santa maria

via corso galileo ferraris

pia solfe

via confienza

corso vittorio emanuele II

via san secondo

via a. massena

corso re umberto

via boucheron

via bertola

via cernaia

caserme cernaia e pietro micca

via a. avogadro

corso

via vinzaglio

via saunaz

corso giacomo matteotti

via san quintino

largo vittorio emanuele II

via magenta

via v. vela

corso stati uniti

stazione porta susa

plazza xvii dicembre

corso inghilterra

N

CONTENTS

INTRODUCTION

TURIN MAY BE THE MOST MISUNDERSTOOD AND UNDERAPPRECIATED CITY IN ITALY. Among Italians the city's reputation is that of a dull and sober provincial outpost blanketed by fog, choked by car exhaust, and surrounded by cement housing blocks straight out of a De Sica film. A Venetian journalist I know calls Turin "austere," a Roman friend finds it "unglamorous," and a friend from Naples claims it might as well be Austria—which is ironic, since many Italians only half-jokingly call it the most Southern city in Italy, given the large number of Southern Italians who have migrated there since the Second World War. The Torinesi themselves are considered uptight, discreet to a fault, perhaps even a touch rude: *falso e cortese* goes the famous Italian saying about them—"false and polite."

Foreigners, too, seem to have a low opinion of Turin, if they think of it at all. It is Fiatville—the "Detroit of Italy"—best seen from the air on the approach to Milan or bypassed altogether. It may have been a stop on the Grand Tour, but even such renowned tourists as Flaubert came away unimpressed—during an 1845 visit he declared it, to paraphrase only slightly, the most boring city in Italy.

It's true that Turin's character has little in common, besides language (and barely that), with the ebullient sunny south of Italy, but what glories these stereotypes, whatever their truth, disguise! Far from being a dull, characterless city, Turin today is casually elegant, but not intimidating; more orderly than most Italian cities, but far from sterile; buoyant, but not boisterous. It is Italy encapsulated, and it is the city I love most.

But why should anyone else? It is beautiful, for one thing. Le Corbusier called Turin the most beautifully set city he had ever seen: nestled between the western Alps and the River Po, it seems as if the city was planned to suit the setting and the scenery—and indeed, it was. There are lovelier rivers than the Po, but where it runs through Turin, it seems to fit right in, and snakes enchantingly around the hills that surround the city. And the buildings that line Turin's long straight streets (a legacy of an early grid put in place by the Romans and carried on by Turin's first city planners) are extraordinary: there are noble palaces, deca-dent cafes, and modernist gems. The grandest of them all, the 530-foot, needle-tipped Mole Antonelliana remains a spectacular sight despite years of over-exposed postcard stardom. From down below the sun glinting off its cupola against the background of the Alps is always a joy to see; and from its spire the view back down to the thousands of red rooftops, over the Po and across Turin's lush hillside is unforgettable. In fact, the hills, dotted with villas and churches and filled with wooded paths, are as much a part of Turin's character as the eleven miles of porticoes that line the streets of the Centro. The French writer Xavier de Mestre, in *A Nocturnal Expedition Around My Room*

(1825), described the view:

> *The hill of Turin on which [Superga] rests gradually*
> *rose before me covered with forests and rich vineyards*
> *displaying its gardens and palaces proudly to the setting*
> *sun. While its simple and modest dwellings seemed half*
> *hidden away in those little valleys serving as a retreat*
> *for the wise man whose meditations they could foster. I*
> *salute you, charming hill! You are painted within my*
> *heart!*

The city is ancient, for another. For anyone with a nose
for history, Turin is a fascinating place to visit. Founded in
Neolithic times by Ligurian tribes who reared sheep for
milk and wool, it was razed to the ground by Hannibal in
218 BC, but revived by Julius Caesar as a Roman settlement
150 years later. It grew slowly until the thirteenth century,
when the ruling Savoy family made Turin the capital of
its expanding kingdom. Over the next few centuries, as
Savoy wealth and power increased, Turin grew in size and
splendor alongside. Conflicts with the French and Spanish
over territory came and went with great consistency and
the French influence bestowed on the city during the Napoleonic years remains vivid. The Savoys were also great
patrons of architecture—their court architects were given
nearly free rein and have, in return, given Turin much of
what makes it so unique.

In the nineteenth century Turin was home to the liberal movement, which culminated in Italian nationhood in 1860 with Turin as its first capital. That soon changed when the capital was abruptly moved to Florence (and then, of course, Rome), leaving Turin filled with the grand buildings appropriate for a national capital. It has also imbued the city with the feeling that something important happened here, but that the men-in-a-hurry have moved on.

In the early twentieth century, Antonio Gramsci came to Turin from Cagliari, the capital of Sardinia, to study, but was soon helping Sardinian immigrants in their efforts to organize labor unions in the auto factories. In a small palazzo in the center of Turin, he established *L'Ordine Nuovo*, which soon became Italy's most influential leftist newspaper. He was arrested and imprisoned in Rome, in 1926, when Mussolini outlawed the Communist Party, and died eleven years later. But his spirit prevailed during the second wave of postwar immigration to the factories and helped make Turin a center for progressive political thought ever since. In April 1945, partisans in Turin who had faced twenty years of Fascist control and then twenty months of German occupation liberated the city from the Nazis after many of its own had died in the struggle on the city's streets. They are movingly memorialized by dozens of small stone plaques, or *lapides*, that line the city's streets collecting flowers and offerings with each mounting anniversary. Even the streets themselves give a sense of the city's illustrious past: they are named after politicians and publishers, scientists and explorers.

Yet for all its history, Turin can feel pleasingly time-less—or at least not of any one time—and it lacks the feeling of being preserved in amber that I find distracting in some other European cities. What others take to be Turin's "austerity" or "severity" I've always found to be a kind of willed aloofness, a pleasing sense of mysterious distraction from the rest of Italy and indeed the rest of the world. As Umberto Eco once wrote "If Turin did not exist, there would be no Italy; but if Italy did not exist, Turin would be exactly the same." The city seems unaware of its own charms; visiting it can feel like a clandestine mission, not least of all because there are rarely many other English-speakers there. Indeed the Torinesi themselves may ask why you've bothered to come, so accustomed to the city's low status among visitors have they become. But one of the pleasures of the place is the ease the Torinesi seem to feel in their own city, and the great pride they take in it once you scratch beneath the surface. Shopkeepers, waitresses, and salespeople are always quick with a recommendation. Still another reason to visit Turin is that it is a cultured city bursting with bookstores, art galleries, and museums. It is where the Italian film industry began, where Italo Calvino, Natalia Ginzburg, Primo Levi, and Cesare Pavese wrote, where Friedrich Nietzsche went mad, and where some of the great names in Italian publishing were established. The state radio and television broadcaster RAI was estab-lished there; the Teatro Alfieri, Teatro Regio, and Teatro Carignano present the best of Italian and international dramatic and musical productions. There are museums devoted to Egyptian artifacts, to nineteenth-century marionettes, and to Alpine picks and hammers. And as a center for contemporary art in Italy, Turin rivals Milan and has inspired key figures in movements as diverse as futurism and *Arte Povera*.

But whatever its architectural charm and cultural sophistication, Turin is at bottom a lived-in city, a place where life happens. It is the city of FIAT and Lancia, home to candy production and textile plants. Much of the industry—and many of the jobs—have long since left, but the city still feels like a city that works, that makes things: chocolate, candy, and coffee are still produced there; a lively group of fashion designers has snubbed Milan in favor of personalized ateliers in up-and-coming neighborhoods; and woodworkers and bookbinders line the quiet streets of the Centro. The French writer Jean Giono, whose father was from the outskirts of Turin, wrote about his new-found passion for the city when he traveled there in 1951. Giono—a famously reluctant traveller—found "nothing attractive about places like Naples and Capri," where the "azure blue bores me as much as the rocks and the flowers"; he preferred Turin, where the buildings lining via Po, he said, reminded him of stage sets (as they still do today, a half-century later) behind which Torinesi families acted out their lives.

Finally, some may find Turin worth visiting just for the pleasures of eating and drinking there. This is a city for gluttony without debauchery: rustic and hearty braised meat dishes are accompanied by sophisticated, deep red wines; creamy risottos are made using local rice and the freshest in-season vegetables; heavily-laden cheese carts highlight local, traditional methods. At the foundation of Turin's robust food culture is the rustic cuisine of the high Alpine valleys and the lower regions of the Langhe and Monferrato hills south of the city, where cheese, rice, and meat dominate. It's possible today to eat well at any price level in Turin, and increasingly possible to eat very good non-Italian food, especially Spanish, Middle Eastern, and North African, but the best local dishes (and most affordable) are to be found in *trattorie* and other family-run establishments that the city abounds in. The Torinesi are particular about their lunch hours and the entire city shuts down between one and three. Even during (the not infrequent) transit strikes, buses and trams will operate on either side of lunchtime to make certain people are able to get home for their afternoon meal and then back to the office. From the pleasures of a simple plate of pasta or a picnic gleaned from market stalls, to *tramezzini* or *panini* at a local cafe or pizza *in passagio*, to a fine four-course lunch, any visitor will be spoiled for choice.

As for wine: there is no finer city in Italy. The product not of the city itself, of course, but of the lush wine growing regions surrounding it, Piedmontese wine is arguably the finest in Italy. Choices range from the product of the noble Nebbiolo grape: the rich Barolo, the somewhat lighter Barbaresco and Langhe Nebbiolo, and the complex Gattinara to the more common—and more affordable—varieties of Barbera, Gavi and Roero (both whites), and the young Grignolino. It is worth noting that vermouth also has a long history in Turin, beginning when Benedetto Carpano opened a vermouth shop near piazza Castello, in 1786, and began producing a liqueur later to be known as Punt e Mes. Martini and Rossi then began making their world famous vermouth in nearby Chieri. Vermouth is still a favorite aperitif in Turin bars.

The great English critic Cyril Connolly once called travel a "neglected art." He wrote that "we cannot dissociate the idea of travelling from the conception of the tourist ... who acquires merit by visiting the leaning Tower. The traveller's interest is subjective, the tourist's objective." This guide is proudly subjective and by no means exhaustive. Rather it intends to provide the discerning traveller—one who loves cities and enjoys being *of* them rather than merely *in* them—a selective inventory of destinations, small discoveries, and itineraries that encourage wandering, focusing on those elements of the city that manifest its culture, history, food, and everyday living.

Every major Italian city (and many minor ones) has Roman ruins, Renaissance churches, numberless piazzas with curly-cue fountains, and charming cobblestone streets to check off the list, but Turin is different. Unlike the rest of Italy, the Renaissance practically bypassed the city and few visual clues of it exist, but thanks to the genius of the city's visionary architects, the city's role as political and cultural capital, and more than a touch of French influence, Turin is part baroque dream, part art nouveau confection. Its broad boulevards in the Parisian style still retain some of the grandeur of their original planning, lined with chestnut trees marked by signs warning: *Attenzione! Castagne cadenti in autunno* ('Watch out! Falling chestnuts in the autumn'). Turin's scale makes it a perfect walking city. While a now-thriving cobbled and winding Roman quarter remains, it is surrounded by a rigid street grid that is unusual for Italy and a *centro storico* (or historic center) as well-preserved as any in Europe, making Turin more manageable than a city like Rome or Milan.

Until now tourism has played only a small role in the city's economy. But with the arrival of the Winter Olympic games in 2006, myriad changes, urban planning initiatives, and improvements are underway. Not all of them are craven attempts at the tourist dollar, and the city seems to be making sincere attempts to better the quality of life for its residents. But there is a palpable tension between "progress" and losing characteristics that are habitual, vital, and unique. I bemoan the loss of the creaking, orange trams from the streets, the attempts to instill some order at Porta Palazzo market, and the inevitable modernization of neglected museum displays, but I also recognize that these are sincere efforts at conservation as much as they are the natural evolution of a thriving city.

In the following pages I've tried to offer recommendations to well-known attractions and to those treasures known only to locals. I have emphasized independently-owned shops and restaurants, artisanal foods, and locally-produced goods wherever possible. I have also included detailed listings of Turin's cultural attractions and personal recommendations to Turin's hotels, restaurants, cafes, and shops. Three guided walks through the city's Roman, Baroque, and modern neighborhoods encompass eating, drinking, architecture, and history. There are suggestions for short trips to nearby towns, ideas for activities if you're travelling with children, and much more. The civilized traveller will find no end to cultural pursuits, epicurean delights, living history, sophisticated shops, and, once under its spell, no end to one of the most understated, most beautiful cities in Italy.

A BRIEF HISTORY
OF TURIN

c. 300 BC	The first Taurini, descendents of Ligurian-Celts and Gallic peoples, settle along the Po river
218 BC	Hannibal crosses the Alps with elephants, invades and levels *Taurasia*
154 BC	Roman legions arrive
58 BC	Julius Caesar establishes *Castra Taurinorum*, a military camp
28 BC	The military camp is expanded into a village, *Augusta Taurinorum*, featuring an orthogonal street grid
69 AD	*Augusta Taurinorum* is burned and nearly destroyed in the civil wars that break out following the death of Nero
398 AD	First cathedral is built

492 AD	Burgundians invade
568 AD	Lombards invade
773 AD	Franks, led by Charlemagne, invade; city becomes part of Carolingian empire
1248 AD	Turin awarded to Tommaso II of Savoy by Emperor Frederick II
1404 AD	University of Turin founded by Ludovico of Savoy
1474 AD	First printing press in Turin
1506 AD	Erasmus obtains degree in theology from University of Turin
1536 AD	French occupy Turin
c. 1550 AD	Population 5,000
1563–1564 AD	Duke Emanuele Filiberto regains control of the city from the French, establishes Turin as Savoy capital
1578 AD	The Holy Shroud brought to Turin from Chambéry

1640 AD	French invade, lay siege to city
1666–1681 AD	The architect Guarino Guarini active in Turin
1706 AD	French again lay siege to city, Pietro Micca sacrifices himself to forestall defeat, and troops led by Prince Eugène of Savoy save the city
1714–1734 AD	The architect Filippo Juvarra active in Turin
1717–1731 AD	Basilica di Superga built to commemorate victory over French
c. 1750 AD	Population 69,000
1763 AD	The cafe Al Bicerin opens
1796 AD	Population 93,000
1798 AD	Vermouth invented in Turin by Antonio Benedetto Carpano
1798 AD	Napoleon's general Joubert occupies Turin; Savoys go into exile

1799 AD	Austro-Russian army defeats French and occupies city
1800–1802 AD	Napoleon defeats Austro-Russian army at Battle of Marengo; Turin annexed to France and city walls torn down
1814–1815 AD	Fall of Napoleon; Congress of Vienna returns Turin to the Savoys
1824 AD	Museo Egizio founded
1853 AD	Railway to Genoa opens
1853 AD	Population 160,000
1861 AD	Kingdom of Italy declared, with Vittorio Emanuele II of Savoy its first king and Turin its first capital
1864 AD	Capital is moved to Florence, and then to Rome in 1870
1871 AD	Frejus Tunnel to Switzerland opens
1875 AD	Caffè Baratti & Milano opens

1881 AD	Population 250,000
1884 AD	World's Fair of Italian Art and Industry is held in Turin
1888–1889 AD	Friedrich Nietzsche's miraculous year in Turin
1897 AD	Juventus football club formed
1889 AD	The Mole Antonelliana is completed after twenty-six years of construction
1899 AD	FIAT founded by Giovanni Agnelli
1902 AD	Second General Italian Exposition, which popularizes the *stile Liberty* (Liberty style), is held in Turin
1906 AD	Torino football club formed
1908 AD	Italy's first moving film company, Società Anonima Ambrosio, formed in Turin
1909 AD	Lancia car group founded by Vincenzo Lancia

1914 AD	Giovanni Pastrone's groundbreaking *Cabiria* filmed in Turin
1920 AD	Antonio Gramsci organizes a general strike in the city's factories
1923 AD	FIAT Lingotto, the largest factory in Europe, opens
1929 AD	Population 500,000
1933 AD	Einaudi publishing firm founded by Giulio Einaudi
1938 AD	Mussolini's race laws implemented across Italy
1939 AD	FIAT Mirafiori, the first mass production factory in Italy, opens
1939–1945 AD	Second World War; Turin heavily bombed, emerges with forty percent of its buildings in rubble and over one thousand factories damaged or destroyed
1943–1945 AD	German occupation of Turin

1945 AD	Partisan uprisings against German occupation
1946 AD	Birth of the Republic of Italy; Savoys go into exile in Portugal
1949 AD	Entire Torino football club dies in an airplane crash on Superga
1950s AD	Mass immigration to Turin from the south, Sardinia, and the Veneto
1951 AD	Population 713,000
1961 AD	Italia '61 Expo in Turin
1961 AD	Population 1,000,000
1982 AD	FIAT Lingotto closes
1987 AD	Primo Levi dies
2001 AD	Population 865,000
2006 AD	Turin hosts winter Olympic games

ART & CULTURE

ONE OF THE GREATEST PLEASURES AND BIG-GEST SURPRISES ABOUT TURIN IS THE sheer variety of museums and cultural activity. Turin is an increasingly serious rival to Milan as the capital of the contemporary art scene in Italy, and it's a deserved reputation: there are countless upstart galleries, august private collectors, and the holdings of the Galleria d'Arte Moderna e Contemporanea (the GAM) in the Crocetta and the Castello di Rivoli, just outside of town, are extraordinary. Turin was not only at the heart of the *Arte Povera* movement in the 1960s, but has been captured on canvas, paper, and film by myriad artists of the twentieth century who have been moved by the atmosphere of the city.

Still, the Renaissance's humanistic spirit did not flourish in Piedmont as it did in other regions of Italy and it is difficult to find evidence in the museums of its local embrace. Small picture galleries, such as the Sabauda and the Pinacoteca at the Accademia Albertina, were royal or academic collections before being opened up to the public and little of their Renaissance holdings were actually produced in the region. Modernism and experimentation both have thrived here and are widely appreciated and exhibited. Turin brims with private art galleries, many concentrated in the bourgeois Borgo Nuovo district, in an up-and-coming area near the Dora River, and in the former factories on via Giulia di Barolo; all feature fine selections of contemporary and early twentieth-century Italian artists not commonly seen elsewhere. If a show is not listed in *Torino Sette* for any of the galleries listed at the end of this section, it may be best to ring before visiting.

Art aside, Turin is rich with rooms dedicated to all aspects of the city's history. Museums and galleries dedicated to cinema (Turin was the home of Italian filmmaking), the unification of Italy (Turin was the first capital of Italy), Egyptology (the second most important collection in the world), and its own industrial production (cars, naturally) mesh seamlessly into the broader web of cultural pursuits.

I highly recommend purchasing a "Torino Card" when you arrive; it is the most economical way of taking in the widest array of the city's museums. It allows free admission to nearly all the major museums and is a bargain at €17 for three day's use. When you purchase one, you'll be given a list of participating museums and a map showing their locations. See the Essentials section for more details.

URLs are given for those museums that maintain their own websites, however, general information for many of the city's museums is available at *www.comune.torino.it/musei*. "Concessions" denotes a discounted entry fee for children, students, senior citizens, etc., and usually requires some proof of status. A star (★) preceding a listing denotes a "must see."

MUSEUMS

★BASILICA DI SUPERGA
Strada della Basilica di Superga, 73 · ☎ 011.899.7456
BASILICA: *9am—12pm daily*
CUPOLA AND SAVOY TOMBS: *9:30am—12pm and 3pm—6pm Mon—Fri; 9:30am—7pm Sat; 1pm—7pm Sun*
Admission: €5; concessions €2
SASSI-SUPERGA RAILWAY: *9am—12pm and 2pm—8pm on the hour Mon, Wed, Thurs, Fri; 9am—8pm on the hour Sat; 7am—12pm on the hour Tues*
Admission: €3.10—€4.13 depending on the day of the week
www.basilicadisuperga.com

Juvarra's genius at work again; an architectural trophy built to celebrate the Savoy's 1706 victory over the French. Construction didn't begin until 1715 and took sixteen years to complete. The magnificent double-shell dome and two belltowers look over the city like a guardian angel. Superga practically glows—its pale yellow exterior seemingly illuminated even on foggy days. King Vittorio Amedeo II had a family crypt installed (designed by Francesco Martinez, Juvarra's nephew); a guided tour is the only way to see it and the peculiar Sala dei Papi—a room whose walls are covered in portraits of 240 popes. Behind the Basilica is the memorial (and a "museum" open only on Sundays) to the celebrated Torino football team of 1949, whose plane crashed here in the fog that May, returning from a friendly match in Lisbon, killing the entire team.

One of the only, and by far the best, ways of getting to Superga is to take a city bus (the number 15 tram or number 61 or 68 bus) to Sassi (meaning "stones": in order to make a level surface at the top of the hill to build upon, the stones cleared from the site were brought here) and board the 1930s single track funicular that climbs the three kilometers up the hill in about 20 minutes. The ride affords miraculous views of the city and the hills. There is a small museum dedicated to the history of Turin's public transport (including the rack railway) at Sassi.

BIBLIOTECA NAZIONALE UNIVERSITARIA
Piazza Carlo Alberto, 3 · ☎ 011.810.1111
Hours: 8:30 am–2:30 pm Mon, Wed, Fri, Sat; 8 am–7 pm Tues, Thur
Admission: free
A passport is required to obtain a reader's card, but no identification is required to see exhibits.
www.bnto.librari.beniculturali.it

Facing Palazzo Carignano across Piazza Carlo Alberto, the Biblioteca Nazionale was established by King Vittorio Amedeo II in 1723 on the site of the Palazzo's stables. The building that houses the library today was built around 1870 by Turin-born Filippo Castelli. Its grand Neo-classicism reflects the decline of the Baroque at this time, and it would have housed the Italian Parliament had the Parliament not been moved to Florence before the building was completed. The King's action merged the holdings of the royal and civic collections and, despite fire and bomb damage, the library's still abundant holdings of illuminated manuscripts, pamphlets, ephemera, and musical scores are regularly the subject of temporary exhibits. To use the library for research, one must apply for a reader's card at the main desk just beyond the entrance.

BIBLIOTECA REALE
Piazza Castello, 191 · ☎ 011.543.885
Hours: 10 am–5 Tues–Sat
Admission: varies depending on exhibit
A passport should be adequate if you want a temporary reader's card, but no identification is required to see exhibits.
The library for the royal family's collection of manuscripts, maps, photographs, and drawings, established by King Carlo Alberto in 1831 and opened in 1837. Open to the public since its founding, Pelagio Palagi's vaulted ceiling and long, parquet-floored room powerfully convey a sense of great history and import. Hours for merely viewing the room are now limited (and seemingly ever-changing), so it is best to check ahead by phone, but researchers can apply for a reader's card. There are occasional exhibits, but it is worth noting that the library is home to the Da Vinci series *Codex on Bird Flight* and the artist's *Self Portrait*, which are viewable if you make a booking in advance.

BORGO E ROCCA MEDIOEVALE

viale Virgilio, 106, Parco del Valentino · ☎ 011.443.1701
BORGO: October–March, 9am–7pm Mon–Sun;
April–September, 9am–8pm Mon–Sun
Admission: free
ROCCA: 9am–7pm Tues–Sun
Admission: €3; concessions €2
www.borgomedioevaletorino.it

The result of a late nineteenth-century revival of interest in the Middle Ages, the *Borgo* (village) and *Rocca* (castle fortress) of the Borgo Medioevale are faithful reproductions of fifteenth-century Piedmontese sites made for the World's Fair of Italian Art and Industry in 1884. The site and buildings were purchased by the city once the Fair ended and became a museum in 1942. It is mildly diverting, especially if you have children in tow, but the real star here is the riverside Parco del Valentino.

CASTELLO DI MONCALIERI

Piazza Baden Baden, 4 (Moncalieri) · ☎ 011.640.2883
Hours: 8:30am–6:30pm Thur, Sat, Sun
Admission: €3; concessions €1.50
www.ambienteto.arti.beniculturali.it

Half museum of furniture, half Carabinieri barracks, the castle still retains some of its medieval feel—parts of the building date to the eleventh century, when it was a fortress (as its formidable position above the Po attests to). The Savoys commissioned Carlo di Castellamonte to transform

augmented Castellamonte's grand plan and fulfilled the
ever-expanding wishes of the Savoy family.

Michelangelo Garove was brought in for "renovations"
in 1699, after the palace had been damaged in a scuffle
with the French six years earlier. In fact, by the time his
plans were adjusted to the French standards that the Savoys
subscribed to, the castle had been completely redesigned
and parts of it torn down to make way for new galleries,
pavillions, and follies. Juvarra took over in 1716, after only
small portion of the colossal Garove project had been realized, and it is his hand that is most visible today. He was
responsible for the castle, the nearby Chiesa di Sant'Uberto
(which has hints of Superga), the *orangerie*, and the stable
complex. After Juvarra died in 1736, Benedetto Alfieri took
the torch, unifying the disparate elements with a long
gallery and the addition of a number of outbuildings used
for storage and livestock. During Napoleon's reign, the
grounds were damaged beyond recognition and the castle
and; they were completely abandoned after World War II.
Now through a huge effort aided by UNESCO, the entire
complex is being restored in an effort to create a mixed-use
cultural destination.

CENTRO STORICO FIAT
Via Chiabrera, 20 · ☎ 011.686.6240
Hours: Open by appointment only; closed on weekends
Admission: free

Founded by the Agnelli family in Turin, in 1899, FIAT, as

it into a Baroque royal residence in 1619; members of the
Savoy family lived in the castle until 1926. Interior decora-
tions by Juvarra and Alfieri are still visible and survived
Nazi occupation during the war.

★CASTELLO DI RIVOLI

Piazza Mafalda di Savoia (Rivoli) · ☎ *011.956.5222*
Hours: 10 am–5 pm Tues–Thurs; 10 am–9 pm Fri–Sun
Admission: €6.50; concessions €4.50; children under 10 free
www.castellodirivoli.org

One of the most unusual and interesting museums of contemporary art in the world. On a hilltop along the old road
to France, the Castello di Rivoli was built by the Savoys
on the ruins of a medieval castle that saw a number of
subsequent additions and renovations beginning in the
early seventeenth century. Many of the greatest architects
active in Piedmont—Ascanio Vittozzi, Carlo di Castellamonte, Michaelangelo Garove, Antonio Bertola, and Filippo
Juvarra—worked on it at some point. In 1693, during the
war with the French, the castle was partially destroyed by
fire. Juvarra's plan should have restored the palace, but the
project—dating to 1718—was never fully completed. Carlo
Randoni was hired in 1793 to carry out Juvarra's design
(a wooden model of which is on display), but it was only
partially complete when Napoleonic troops occupied the
building just a few years later. In subsequent decades the
unfinished castle became a financial and practical burden to
the Savoy family, who sold the buildings to the city in 1883.

Over time they were put into service as barracks, barns, and warehouses. In the 1970s the regional government decided to transform it into a new museum of contemporary art. The architect Andrea Bruno's design cleverly incorporated the unfinished parts using modern materials in the grand Baroque space, and the museum was opened in 1984. Great windows mark the end of the *manica lunga*—originally intended as a picture gallery, and now used for temporary shows—and a small glass observation box juts out unexpectedly from the side of the castle overlooking the brick piazza. Inside, the atmosphere is wonderfully strange. The museum boasts a stellar selection of works from the *Arte Povera* movement of the 1960s, which sprung from urban centers affected by the economic downfall of the time. *Arte Povera* ("poor art") artists worked outside formal definitions of artmaking and form, used everyday materials, and incorporated the viewer into the piece. It was a wildly influential period and industrial, economically stricken Turin was its natural home.

In addition to holding a wide range of major works by contemporary artists from all over the world in its permanent collection, it hosts important travelling exhibits. Much of the art is displayed in barren castle rooms with their evocatively fading painted decorations, mouldings, and parquet floors still intact. Among the highlights are: Mario Merz's neon *Manica Lunga da 1 a 987* along the exterior of the building; Maurizio Cattelan's *Novocento*, a stuffed horse hanging from a Baroque painted ceiling by slings;

Giuseppe Penone's memorable *Respirare l'ombr*
lined with chicken-wire filled with hundreds
of bay leaves; and a room of Alighiero Boet
woven maps from the 1970s. You can travel
the number 36 bus from Piazza Statuto, a
trip. Walk up the winding hill streets to th
dominates the town. On the way, peek into
dens of decadent and decaying art nouveau
the piazza in front of the museum, enjoy th
view—the castle was built to be perfec
Superga, visible on a clear day.

CASTELLO REGGIA DI VENARI
Piazza della Repubblica, 4 (Venaria Re
Hours: 9 am–11:30 pm and 2:30 pm–5 pn
by appointment
Admission: €3, guided tours only
www.reggiavenariareale.it
The most ambitious of the Savoys' h
Reale—once considered the Versa
located about two miles outside th
number 72 and a short walk). Beg
te's grand architectural vision—
Diana—took sixteen years to re
village, elaborate gardens (whi
and the palace itself, the Reg
renovated, upgraded, and adde
Reale bears the marks of three

the old saying goes, "is Turin and Turin is Italy." Inextricably linked with the industrial, economic, and political history of the country, FIAT (which stands for Fabbrica Italiana Automobili Torino) had a mere thirty-five employees in 1902 when they produced their first car. In 1916, they had a state-of-the-art plant at Lingotto, then the largest factory in Italy. It employed 50,000 people when World War II broke out and operated to full capacity for military purposes. Today, the company still makes cars, of course, and has taken up production for other makers, but employs a fraction of the number it did in its prime.

South of the Parco del Valentino and near the Po, this private museum displays models, drawings, photographs, advertising ephemera, and a deconstructed FIAT Mefistofele (which broke a speed record in 1923). There is also a section dedicated to FIAT's work in the aeronautical industry, a library, and an archive. Look for the low-slung Liberty building with the stone "FIAT" relief along the top.

FIAT FACTORY TOUR
corso Giovanni Agnelli, 200 · ☎ *06.003.4269*
Admission: free

A free tour of the Mirafiori factory can be arranged (and is available in English), but only by appointment, and no photography is allowed inside the plant. At three million square meters, it was one of the largest factories in the world when it opened. Designed by the engineer Vittorio Bonadé-Bottino, its May 1939 opening was presided over by Mussolini. At its height Mirafiori employed over 60,000 people, many from Italy's deep south who immigrated north for jobs and, as a result, realized the country's post-war "economic miracle"; in the economic decline and political unrest of the 1970s the plant was the site of violent strikes. Today, it employs about 16,000 people (39% of whom are women) and manufactures Alfa Romeos, Maseratis, and Lancias, among others.

FONDAZIONE ACCORSI MUSEO DI ARTI DECORATIVE
via Po, 55 · ☎ 011.812.9116
Hours: 10am–8pm Tues, Wed, Fri–Sun; 10am–11pm Thurs
Admission: €6.50–€8; concessions €5–€6.50, depending on exhibit
www.fondazioneaccorsi.it

Pietro Accorsi's astounding collection of furniture and decorative arts, incuding rugs, tapestries, and *objets d'art* is arranged in this 1684 Castellamonte-designed palace as if Accorsi himself had just stepped out for the paper. Unfashionable when he began collecting, his taste for eighteenth-century items has led to perhaps the finest decorative art collection in Italy.

Accorsi was raised in a modest apartment in the palazzo when his father was a caretaker here. He later rented part of the building himself, and then purchased the entire premises in 1956. Following his death the palazzo became the headquarters of his foundation and, in 1999, a museum. Look for listings of classical music performances and lectures held in the richly decorated rooms.

FONDAZIONE MERZ
via Limone, 24 · ☎ 011.197.19437
Hours: 11am–7pm Tues–Sun
Admission: €5; concessions €3.50
www.fondazionemerz.org

In 2004–2005, the Lancia car factory's former heating plant was stripped and transformed into the perfect white cube setting for Mario Merz's sculptures and early paintings. In a semi-industrial part of San Paolo, not far from the Fondazione Sandretto Re Rebaudengo, the unassuming building has three floors (plus outdoor space) dedicated to the artist's "igloos," neon sculptures, and paintings. Eventually the Fondazione plans to hold temporary shows and incorporate a bookshop and cafe, but for now the atmosphere is quiet and contemplative. The enthusiastic guards shadow visitors a little too vigorously, but for those interested in Merz's work, the gallery doesn't disappoint.

FONDAZIONE SANDRETTO RE REBAUDENGO
via Modane, 16 · ☎ 011.1983.1600
Hours: Tues, Wed, Fri–Sun 12pm–8pm; Thurs 12pm–11am
Admission: €5; concessions €3; free on Thursdays
www.fondsrr.org

Since 1995, the Fondazione Sandretto Re Rebaudengo has organized cultural events and contemporary art exhibits from its orginal home near Cuneo, the Palazzo Re

Rebaudengo. The Turin space was established in 2002, in the working class San Paolo neighborhood. Designed by architect Claudio Silvestrin, the long, low gallery is carved out of a former factory building. A third of the complex is given over to neutral exhibition space with an additional gallery specifically for video installations. Concerts, lectures, and dance programs associated with special exhibitions are also held in these spaces. There is a small bookshop and a popular cafe and restaurant, Spazio, designed by Rudolf Stingel.

★GALLERIA CIVICA D'ARTE MODERNA E CONTEMPORANEA (GAM)
via Magenta, 31 · ☎ 011.562.9911
Hours: 9am–7pm Tues–Sun (bookshop 10am–7pm)
Admission: €7.50; €4 concessions; free on Thursdays
www.gamtorino.it

Turin was the first Italian city to collect and exhibit contemporary art as a civic measure and since 1895 its collections have been housed on this site; but the museum's current building, designed by Carlo Bassi and Goffredo Boschetti, opened in 1959. With a concentration in Italian art—the older part of the collection in Piedmontese art in particular—the museum is divided between two floors. The one focused on the nineteenth century features Fontanesi landscapes, a room of Carlo Bossoli's scenes of Turin from the 1860s, including *Veduta ideale del Po a Torino*, his fantastical image of the river in full springtime flush with an island folly in the middle and a promenade along the shore; and the *Processione del Corpus Domini*, an 1847 scene of via Garibaldi that looks surprisingly like the thoroughfare today. One of my favorite depictions of Turin is Enrico Reycend's *Lungo il Po, presso la Gran Madre di Dio a Torino* (c 1882), an almost Seurat-like river scene. The twentieth-century collection features, in addition to a fine range of *Arte Povera* pieces, important works by Italians such as Casorati, Modigliani, Morandi, and De Chirico (including his haunting 1940 self-portrait), as well as major works by important modernists, such as Dix, Klee, and Picabia. Other highlights include Torinese Paolo Mussat Santor's exceptional *Ritratti di artista* portrait series; *Le Suore*, by Asti native Mino Rosso; and *Aeropittura*—a beautiful piece by Futurist Nicolaj Diulgheroff, who called Turin home.

★GALLERIA SABAUDA
via Accademia delle Scienze, 6 · ☎ 011.547.440
Hours: Nov−May, 8:30 am−2 pm Tues, Fri−Sun; 2 pm−7:30 pm Wed; 10 am−7:30 pm Thurs
June−Oct, 8:30 am−2 pm Tues, Fri−Sun; 2 pm−7:30 pm Wed−Thurs
Admission: €4; concessions €2 (combined ticket with Museo Egizio €8)
www.artito.arti.beniculturali.it
Amidst the steady procession of Savoy portraits and altarpieces, which can become a tad monotonous, are some stunners. This very pleasant space is both world renowned

and loved by the Torinesi. Circulation through the near-silent galleries can be confusing, but the rooms are well lit, contemplative spaces, and the main stairwell is a beautiful piece of design. Some of my favorites are the anonymous portrait of Petrarch; Hans Memling's *Passion of Christ*; the *Portrait of a Sleeping Man* attributed to Rembrandt; Gentileschi's *Annunciation*; Bogetti's *Tempesta con Nefraugio*; and Giulio Clovio's *Four Scenes from the Passion*. Of special note, however, is the Gualino collection of small Etruscan and Greco-Roman pieces, and the startling *Girolamo nel deserto* by Benvenuto di Giovanni, an otherworldly, Dalí-esque portrayal from the late fifteenth century of Jerome in his Syrian desert solitude, loyal lion at his side.

LAVAZZA FACTORY TOUR
strada Settimo, 410 (Settimo Torinese) · ☎ *011.239.8500*
For over 100 years, Lavazza has been making coffee in Turin. Cafes throughout the city boast the blue Lavazza logo and tens of thousands of Torinesi (indeed, Italians!) drink their coffee daily. A short way out of the city center is Lavazza's coffee processing plant; it is possible to visit if you make an appointment in advance.

MUSEO ARMERIA REALE

Piazza Castello, 191 · ☎ 011.543.889
Hours: 1:30pm–7:30pm Tues, Thurs; 9am–2pm Sat–Sun
Admission: €4
www.artito.arti.beniculturali.it

The royal armory, founded by King Carlo Alberto in 1837, is located next door to the Biblioteca Reale. The *armeria* displays a dizzying array of weapons and armor culled from the arsenals of Turin and Genoa, augmented by subsequent contributions to the collection. Highlights are Napoleon's sword, suits of armor that display incredible workmanship and artistic embellishment, and a collection of Turkish, Persian, and Chinese weapons.

MUSEO CIVICO D'ARTE ANTICA

Palazzo Madama, Piazza Castello · ☎ 011.442.9931
Call for new times and admission on reopening

Recently renovated, the Museo Civico d'Arte Antica features a remarkable collection of works—almost unknown outside of Italy—by Piedmontese masters: paintings, illuminated manuscripts, tapestries, ceramic pieces, and altar-pieces. The jewel of the collection, however, is *Les tres riches heures de Milan*, a book illustrated by Jan van Eyck. The museum entrance is located in the Juvarra facade of Palazzo Madama, where one can also take in his unique scissor staircase in the atrium.

MUSEO CIVICO PIETRO MICCA

via Guicciardini, 7/a · ☎ 011.546.317
Hours: 9am–7pm Tues–Sun
Admission: €3

Pietro Micca, a legendary figure in Piedmont, was a twenty-nine-year-old soldier when, during the War of Spanish Succession, the French army lay siege to Turin for four months in 1706. From nine miles of underground tunnels beneath the Cittadella, Torinese patriots tried to keep the French at bay. In an attempt to keep one French battalion from breaking into the citadel, Pietro Micca lit the fuse for a mine, which forestalled the French, but also killed him in the process. His sacrifice (whether deliberate or not is the cause of historical debate) marked the end of the siege and his name has lived on, half in history, half in legend. The museum, which doesn't appear to have been updated since its 1961 opening, displays some interesting maps of the seventeenth-century city and a scale model of Turin before the siege. Call in advance to book a guided tour in the tunnels; tours are not available in English.

MUSEO DEL TESSILE

via Demaria, 10 (Chieri) · ☎ 011.942.7421
Open by appointment only
Admission: free
www.fondazionetessilchieri.com

In the pretty hill town of Chieri (a winding twenty-five minute ride on the number 30 bus from Piazza Vittorio

Veneto), this relatively new museum, in the former convent of Santa Chiara, commemorates the town's history as a center of weaving, dyeing, and cotton, silk, wool, and linen production. On display are fabrics, documents, and sample books, but looms (one dating to the early part of the sixteenth century) take pride of place here. Chieri was also known for its indigenous indigo dye, extracted from a local plant called *gualdo*. Though the last of the dye houses in Chieri closed in the 1960s, the town is still home to a number of cotton and synthetic fabric mills. See page 185 in the *Excursions* section for more about Chieri.

MUSEO DELLA MARIONETTA
via Santa Teresa, 5 · ☎ 011.532.0238
Open by appointment only or during performances
Admission: €2.60; performances around €5

One of the most surprising and pleasing small museums anywhere, the Museo della Marionetta is accessed through an unpromising doorway into a basement next door to the church of Santa Teresa. Open only by appointment or when the Gianduja Theater is staging a performance, the Lupi family's 5,000-piece collection of marionettes, costumes, stage sets, and ephemera date from the troupe's early days in Turin in the 1800s. Among the pieces on display are a puppet-sized Turin tram, an eight-member brass band of chickens, the full cast of *Aida*, and a display of puppet-sized hats.

MUSEO DELLA SANTA SINDONE (MUSEUM OF
THE HOLY SHROUD)
via San Domenico, 28 · ☎ 011.436.5832
Hours: 9am–12pm and 3am–7pm Mon–Sun
Admission: €5.50; €4.50 concessions

The Holy Shroud of Turin—known here as the Sacra Sindone—is believed by some to be the length of cloth Christ
was wrapped in after being removed from the cross. Its
journey to Turin is murky, to say the least, and technically
it can be traced only to the middle ages, but it is said to
have been donated to Savoy family when they still resided
in Chambéry, and moved with them to Turin in 1578; since
then it has been a source of controversy, wonder, and devotion. (The Shroud is actually held in a multi-layered casket
at the Duomo (see page 79) and has been displayed only
on rare occasions—every twenty-five years or so—at the
discretion of the Vatican. However, there is no shortage of
replicas on display here.) Whatever you believe about its
origins, once you get beyond the stilted and didactic film
and the guided tour of the underwhelming Santa Sindone
church, an exhibit showcasing the history of and cult-like
devotion to the Shroud is informative and fascinating.
Housed in the vaulted crypt of the church, the exhibit is
well-presented and takes the visitor on a scientific tour of
the Shroud's history, including the enormous camera used
to take the first photographs of the Shroud in 1898 and a
variety of devotional mementoes.

MUSEO DELL'AUTOMOBILE

corso Unità d'Italia, 40 · ☎ 011.677.666
Hours: 10am–6:30pm Tues–Wed, Fri–Sat; Thurs 10am–
10pm; 10am–8:30pm Sun
Admission: €5.50; concessions €4
www.museoauto.it

Befitting the home of the Italian car industry, Turin's auto museum boasts around 160 vintage cars and models. While the building, opened in 1960, is a treasure of Italian modernism and suits the nature of the museum, the drab interiors and the displays could do with a little updating.

★MUSEO DI ANTICHITÀ

via XX Settembre, 88/C · ☎ 011.521.2251
Hours: 8:30am–7:30pm Tues–Sun
Admission: €4; concessions €2
www.museitorino.it/museoantichita/index.html

Undervisited and overshadowed by the popular Museo Egizio, the Museo di Antichità is wonderfully set in the redesigned former greenhouses of the Palazzo Reale. Many of the artifacts on dispay reveal the rich Bronze Age, pre-Roman, and Roman lives of *Augusta Taurinorum* and surrounding Piedmont sites. Highlights include a surprising collection of ancient glass, Greek vases and statuary, pristine Roman-era silver from Piedmont, and a notable collection of Etruscan bronzes and urns. A new gallery dedicated to the earliest history of the city is due to open soon.

MUSEO DI ARTE E AMMOBILIAMENTO PALA-
ZZINA DI CACCIA DI STUPINIGI (NICHELINO)
Piazza Principe Amedeo, 7 · ☎ 011.358.1220
Hours: Nov—Mar, 9 am—5 pm Tues—Sun;
Apr—Oct, 10 am—6 pm Tues—Sun
Admission: €6.20; concessions €5.20

The furniture museum that has been installed in the royal
hunting lodge at Stupinigi, a twenty-five minute bus ride
from the center of Turin, is delightfully dusty and a tad
down at the heel, which is not to say that the impressive
Juvarra *palazzina* isn't worth a visit. To call this a "little
palace" is a great understatement. The center structure of
the star-shaped, multi-winged hunting "lodge" is capped
by a dome, further topped by a larger than life-size stag.
Damaged by German troops during the occupation and
later restored, the collection at Stupinigi suffered the later
indignity, in 2001, of being looted; many fine examples of
Italian and French furniture and decorative art are still
missing. Wending your way through, the Eastern Apartment has remarkable architectural frescoes by Giovanni
Battista Alberoni (room 13) and a Wedgewood-like cup-
board by the Torinese Franceso Bolgié. Towards the end of
the tour through the building, the simple chambers—by
comparison to the rest of the palace—of King Carlo Felice
feature beautiful ceilings by Giovanni Pietro and the
absurdly immodest canopy beds topped with crowns (rooms
39 and 43). The vaulted stables surrounding the castle often
host travelling art exhibitions and are themselves beau-

tiful structures. If taking public transit—the number 41 bus from Turin goes there—note that you should catch the return bus at the same stop at which you alighted for the palace; the driver should announce the change for the Turin-bound bus, in the small town of Borgaretto, but to avoid a tour around the suburbs, let the driver know when you board that you are headed back to the city.

MUSEO DIFFUSO DELLA RESISTENZA, DELLA DEPORTAZIONE, DELLA GUERRA, DEI DIRITTI, E DELLA LIBERTÀ

Corso Valdocco, 4/a · ☎ 011.436.1433
Hours: 10am–6pm Tues–Sun
Admission: free
www.istoreto.it

The museum's mouthful of a name belies its straightforward mission to disseminate the history of the Resistance in Turin and the deportations from the city during World War II through pictures and film. Relatively new and still finding its bearings, the ground and second floor displays are a little light on explanatory text, and utilize photographs in an overly simplistic way. However, the temporary exhibits and film events around the subjects of resistance, war, and liberty from a global perspective, have been popular, and draw from the richest parts of the museum's archive. The building is a Juvarra-designed barracks from the 1720s that, at the time, also functioned as the western gate to the city. For more about the Resistance movement in Turin, see page 65.

★MUSEO EGIZIO
via Accademia delle Scienze, 6 · ☎ 011.561.7776
Hours: 8:30am−7:30pm Tues−Sun
Admission: €6.50; concessions €2 (combined ticket with
Galleria Sabauda €8)
www.museitorino.it/museoegizio/index.html

Widely hailed as the most significant collection of Egyptian artifacts outside of Cairo, the Museo Egizio is one of the cultural highlights of any trip to Turin. Its rich holdings were formed by a combination of King Carlo Felice's purchase of Bernardino Drovetti's personal collection (assembled while he was Napoleon's consul in Egypt and made famous by Jean-François Champollion's use of it in his groundbreaking work deciphering Egyptian hieroglyphics) in 1824 and the excavations of the Schiaparelli and Farina expeditions during the Italian "Missione Archaeologica" in the early twentieth century. The exhibition begins with 4th- and 5th-dynasty artifacts—wood statues, terracotta bowls, and calcite beakers, and continues into the well-designed lower level remarkable not only for the tomb of Iti and the hoard of pottery, statuary, and alabaster funerary jars from Qau el Kabir, but for the incorporation into the gallery of Turin's Roman wall. The entire collection is a fascinating display. Smaller exhibits throughout the building feature correspondence and documentation related to the Schiaparelli excavation; papyrus and textiles; a wooden model of

Nefertiti's tomb; and the remarkable statue of King Seti of Karnak. The long, bright upstairs halls of the Accademia delle Scienze make ideal galleries for large statuary and steles.

★MUSEO NAZIONALE DEL CINEMA
via Montebello, 20 · ☎ 011.812.5658
Hours: 9am–8pm Tues–Fri, Sun; 9am–11pm Sat
Admission: Combined ticket for museum and panoramic lift
€6.80, concession €5.20; museum only €5.20,
concession €4.20; panoramic lift only €3.62,
concession €2.58; Children under 10, free.
www.museonazionaledelcinema.org

Turin was where the celebrated Italian film industry began in 1904, and with this structure the city finally has the museum it deserves. Housed in what has become the postcard symbol of Turin—the Mole Antonelliana—the Museo Nazionale del Cinema was opened in 2001. In an ambitious and imaginative repurposing of a building, the addition of a glass-enclosed elevator to an observation deck provides a dizzying trip through the 164-foot high dome to 360° views of the city below and the Alps beyond. The incomparable collection of cinema-related artifacts is divided into sections covering stage sets, scripts, actors and actresses, soundtracks, and so on. There is also a circular gallery of movie posters. One could spend an entire visit just in the Archeology of Cinema section, which tells the story of the origins of film and features preserved (and working examples of) precursors to cinema, including a camera obscura, panoramas and peep shows, zoetropes, stereoscopes, panopticons, and early photographs (including the first photographs taken of Turin). Deliriously fun stuff. A ramp wends you up along the side of the dome into the other exhibits, most of which, naturally, have films accompanying them. On the main floor is a theater-like set up of reclining chairs from which you can watch two large screens showing film depictions of Italy—from the early days of Turin's silent film industry to the neo-realism many people have come to associate with post-war Italy. A trip to the Museo del Cinema is pure delight for adults and children alike. (Note that across the street at via Verdi, 18, is the excellent independent Massimo Cinema, a rep house screening new Italian and European releases and classic American movies in English.)

★MUSEO NAZIONALE DEL RISORGIMENTO
via Accademia delle Scienze, 5 · ☎ 011.562.1147
Hours: 9am–7pm Tues–Sun
Admission: €5; concessions €3.50
www.regione.piemonte.it/cultura/risorgimento

The germ of the idea for a unified Italy—or at least a unified nationalistic spirit—can be traced to Napoleon's reign of the Kingdom of Italy in the very early 1800s. On his fall in 1814, the idea, rather than diminish, became a celebrated cause among the intelligentsia and monarchs wary of losing their political station. Though patriots from all over Italy were involved in the quest for Italian unification, Piedmont—and northern Italy, generally—was literally on the frontlines of the biggest threats to nationhood (France and Austria), and was the heart of the Risorgimento movement. Four men are most often celebrated as heroes of the Risorgimento—though they didn't always work in concert: politician (and failed painter) Massimo d'Azeglio; naval captain (and wildman) Giuseppe Garibaldi; intellectual (and editor of the newspaper *Il Risorgimento*) Camillo Cavour; and lawyer and populist Giuseppe Mazzini. Italy was in a state of total revolution between 1848 (the beginning of a war with Austria) and 1861 (when the first national parliament met in Palazzo Carignano).

This period is exhaustively uncovered in the museum's twenty-six room tour of Italy's slow march toward nationhood and its post-unification tensions, including sections devoted to World War I and the annexation of Trieste and Trento, Fascism, and the the divisive resistance movement during World War II. In addition to documents, paintings, banners, weapons, maps, and photographs, the museum also incorporates the chambers of the Sub-Alpine Parliament, where the new leaders of Italy would have met had the capital of the country not been moved to Florence before it was completed in 1871. The palazzo, built between 1679 and 1684 by Guarino Guarini for Prince Emanuele Filiberto (who was, incidentally, deaf and dumb) as a residence, is as richly decorated inside with ornamental stucco, carvings, and frescoes (beautifully preserved; make sure to look up as you walk through the exhibition), as the exterior is with propeller- and star-shaped designs in brick—during construction, Guarini had a kiln set up a few blocks away to make the custom-shaped bricks. The front is adorned with an elaborate escutcheon, added in 1884, dedicated to the birth at the palazzo of Vittorio Emanuele II. In 1799 Napoleon installed his regional government in the palazzo, and in subsequent years it housed the State Council, regional administration, and the Central Post Office before becoming home to the Museo del Risorgimento in 1938. An archive holds original documents belonging to the foremost figures of the Risorgimento: Cavour, Garibaldi, and Mazzini, in addition to a complete run of the newspaper *La Gazzetta del Popolo*—an invaluable resource of Italian political history and journalism.

★MUSEO NAZIONALE DELLA MONTAGNA
DUCA DEGLI ABRUZZI
via Giardino, 39 · ☎ 011.660.4104
Hours: 9am–7pm Mon–Sun
Admission: €5; concessions €3.50
www.museomontagna.org

Situated above the city on Monte dei Cappuccini, the Museo Nazionale della Montagna provides the best view of the Alps without actually heading to the mountains. The museum was established by the Turin branch of the climbing organization, Club Alpino Italiano. In 1874 the city agreed to allow the club to install a *Vedetta Alpina* (Alpine observatory) on Monte dei Cappuccini, comprising a simple pavilion and mobile telescope on the grounds beside the Capuchin monastery. In 1877, the observation post was moved inside and rooms were added to contain a growing collection of mountaineering gear and ephemera. The panoramic room, with a map keyed to all the visible peaks of the western Alps, takes in the breathtaking scope of the mountains, and is the best place from which to see the city nestled in its splendid setting. The museum reopened after a lengthy restoration in 1942, only to be seriously damaged during an air raid the following year. Today the museum is considered the most important of its kind and in addition to a permanent collection that details the environmental aspects of mountains and mountaineering the world over, the museum holds a vast documentary collection and archive, along with a collection of historical films on climbing. Appropriately, a bit of a climb is required to reach the museum—but only up a paved hillside road. (The museum also administers the Exilles fort in the Susa Valley and the Gastaldi Mountain Shelter Museum on Crot del Ciaussiné in Balme—located in a mountain refuge built in 1880. Weather conditions dictate the opening times, so be sure to call before visiting, 0122.58270.)

MUSEO REGIONALE DI SCIENZE NATURALI AND MUSEO DI ZOOLOGIA

via Giolitti, 26 · ☎ 011.432.07332
Hours: 10am–7pm Tues–Sun
Admission: €5; concessions €2.50
www.regione.piemonte.it/museoscienzenaturali

The jointly-run natural science and zoology museum has not yet caught up with the interactive bells-and-whistles approach of such museums in other cities and can sometimes be eerily quiet and empty. But what they lack in clearly presented information and interactive display, they more than make up for in oddball charm. In the natural science museum, there are displays about local flora and fauna and a captivating room of gems and minerals. But the real jewel is the adjacent zoological museum of hundreds of taxidermy animals displayed in a cavernous room on bulging, ribbed wood shelves—a mirror of the enormous whale skeleton that shares the room. This is the animal kingdom at your fingertips, with no glass enclosures (nor explanatory labels), and a walk through the halls is a powerful reminder of the beauty of the animal world. In warm months, musical events are sometimes held in the museum's enclosed court-yard.

MUSEO STORICO NAZIONALE DELL'ARTIGLIERIA AND CITTADELLA

Corso Galileo Ferraris, 0 · ☎ *011.562.9223*
Hours: 8:30 am – 1 pm Tues, Thurs, Sun
Admission: free

Turin's primary fortress, built between 1564–1566, was commissioned by Emanuele Filiberto to protect the city — and his family's rule — from the mounting French threat. It has operated as a quasi-museum since 1733, though it still defended the city as late as 1799. In the 1850s, most of the enormous structure (which once reached to Porta Susa station, five long blocks away) was knocked down in order to facilitate westward development. All that stands today is the main gate, pretty imposing in itself, which houses a collection of heavy artillery from Napoleonic times to the First World War, regimental flags and banners, and a lot of lances, halbards, and bayonets. Strictly for dedicated weapons buffs.

ORTO BOTANICO

viale Mattioli, 25 · ☎ *011.661.2447*
Hours: 9 am – 1 pm and 3 pm – 7 pm Sat – Sun
Admission: €3; concessions €1.50
www.bioveg.unito.it/ortoita/ortob.htm

Small but lovely, and especially worth a visit if you're wandering through the Parco Valentino. Founded in 1729 to cultivate herbal medicinal bases, the garden today has an *orangerie*, a herbarium, and a hothouse. There is also a collection of Alpine plants in the *giardino roccioso* and a "Bible garden" planted with species mentioned in the good book. The Orto Botanico gets special mention for having a guided route through the garden developed specifically for the visually impaired.

PALAZZO BRICHERASIO

via Lagrange, 20 · ☎ *011.571.1811*
Hours: 3 pm–11 pm Mon; 11 am–11 pm Tues–Sun, during exhibits only
Admission: €6.50; concessions €4.50
www.palazzobricherasio.it

Built in 1636 and owned by the Bricherasio family since 1855, this handsome palazzo was until recently the home of Luigi Cacherano di Bricherasio and his two art-loving children. They have now established an exhibition space for modern and contemporary art, and host three or four exhibitions a year; look for posters announcing the shows or in the listings section of *Torino Sette*.

PINACOTECA DELL'ACCADEMIA ALBERTINA DELLE BELLE ARTI

via Accademia Albertina, 8 · ☎ *011.817.7862*
Hours: 9 am–1 pm and 3 pm–7 pm Tues–Sun
Admission: €4; concessions €2.60
www.accademialbertina.torino.it

The pinacoteca, or picture gallery, at the fine arts academy was established in the 1820s as a teaching gallery based on the

200-piece collection of the Archibishop, and later enhanced by King Carlo Alberto's collection of sixteenth-century drawings. All of this is on display to this day, along with works from Italian and Dutch masters. After years of sitting somewhat idle and a lengthy restoration process, the pinacoteca displays splendid works in a peaceful setting, while still retaining an academic flavor, and visitors sometimes have the quiet galleries to themselves. My favorites here are the two Guglielmo Caccia Madonnas; the Turin-born Ludovico Raymond's dark *Sacrilegio*; the Nicasius Bernaerts still-lifes; a room dedicated to floral and architectural studies, and the King's Renaissance cartoons by Gaudenzio Ferrari, Gerolamo Giovenone, and Bernadino Lanino.

PINACOTECA GIOVANNI E MARELLA AGNELLI

via Nizza, 230 · ☎ *011.006.2713*
Hours: 9am–7pm Tues–Sun
Admission: €4; concessions €2.50
www.pinacoteca-agnelli.it

Housed at the top of the former FIAT Lingotto factory, and extending into a new structure designed by Renzo Piano in 2002, this light-flooded jewelbox gallery houses the Agnelli's rather unadventurous roster of paintings from the usual suspects: Canaletto, Matisse, Manet, Renoir. However, Picasso's *Homme appuyé sur une table*, Gino Severini's *Lanciers italiens au galop*, and Giacomo Balla's *Velocità astratta* are notable here, and worth visiting, especially if one of the gallery's smart temporary exhibitions is up.

GALLERIES

ALBERTO PEOLA ARTE CONTEMPORANEA
via della Rocca, 29 · ☎ 011.812.4460

BIASUTTI E BIASUTTI
via Bonafus, 7/L · ☎ 011.817.3511

CARBONE.TO
via dei Mille, 38 · ☎ 011.839.5911

FRANCO MASOERO
via Giulia di Barolo, 13 · ☎ 011.885.933

GALLERIA WEBER
via San Tommaso, 7 · ☎ 011.812.3519

GIORGIO PERSANO
Piazza Vittorio Veneto, 9 · ☎ 011.835.527

PAOLO TONIN GALLERY
Via San Tommaso, 6 · ☎ 011.197.10514

PHOTO & CONTEMPORARY
via Dei Mille, 36 · ☎ 011.899.8884

SONIA ROSSO
via Giulia di Barolo 11/h · ☎ 011.817.2478

ARCHITECTURE

TURIN'S UNIQUE ARCHITECTURAL CHAR-
ACTER, WITHOUT DOUBT, DERIVES LARGELY
from the surviving work of Baroque visionaries and court
architects to the Savoy family, Guarino Guarini, Filippo
Juvarra, and Carlo di Castellamonte (the only Turin native
of the three), whose work is widely discussed throughout
other parts of this book. But the city's architectural cham-
pions also made Turin a laboratory of styles and a seat of
experiment and progress.

Industry, of course, made an impact on the growth of
modernism in and around the city. Given Turin's strong
association with the excesses of the Baroque, some of the
city's curious works of modern architecture may even come
as a surprise, but the movement was readily embraced in
the first half of the twentieth century.

Apart from the architectural jewels mentioned elsewhere in the book—especially those you'll encounter along
the Walks—below are recommended clusters of styles that
appear throughout the city.

VIGNE

With a good map (and the numbers 73 and 54 buses), some
notable hillside *vigne* in La Collina are worth visiting (note
that these are—almost without exception—private buildings, which you will only be able to view from the street):

- Villa Abegg, *strada Comunale San Vito Revigliasco, 65*
- Villa Rey, *strada Comunale Superiore Val San Martino, 27*
- Villa Paradiso, *strada Comunale Superiore Val San Martino, 137*
- Villa Musy, *strada Valpiana, 83/87*

ECLECTICISM AND STILE LIBERTY
...IN THE CENTRO

The eclectic style in architecture emerged in Turin around 1820 and bucked the traditional theory of composing buildings based on historical themes or according to their purpose. It was a popular movement that lasted around seventy-five years and even re-emerged prior to World War I. With a more naturalistic approach, stylistic components from different schools of architecture were combined and original results abounded. For reasons of era and geography, it is no wonder that many examples of eclecticism in Turin combine baroque and neo-classical styles while embracing the organic forms of art nouveau. Some of the key examples of eclectic public buildings and churches are in and around the Centro.

- Palazzo Ceriana, *Piazza Solferino, 11*
- Casa Reda, *via San Francesco d'Assisi, 15*
- Stazione Porta Nuova, *Piazza Carlo Felice*
- Chiesa San Secondo, *via San Secondo, 8*

- Palazzo Priotti, *Corso Vittorio Emanuele II, 52*
- Chiesa Evangelica Valdese, *Corso Vittorio Emanuele II, 23*
- Chiesa di San Giovanni Evangelista, *Corso Vittorio Emanuele II, 13*

. . . IN PIAZZA CRIMEA

The Art Nouveau movement was dubbed *Stile Liberty* in Italy and, in Turin, was embraced by the upper middle class who, as they moved out of the crowded city center into the foothills of La Collina (known as the *pre-collina*), could afford to commission elaborately decorated homes and apartment buildings that bridged the popular eclectic movement with the suddenly popular Liberty style. While the influence of eclecticism and art nouveau can be felt throughout the city, some of the best residential examples can be found close to the east bank of the river and south of Capucine, where Ponte Umberto I empties into Piazza Crimea.

- Casa Bellia, *Corso Fiume, 11*
- Villa Treves, *via Bezzecca, 11*
- Casa Camusso-Caselli, *Corso Fiume, 2*
- Villa Gelati, *via Gatti, 24*

. . . IN THE CROCETTA AND CITTADELLA

The long straight boulevards of the Crocetta and Cittadella are lined with stately apartment buildings built around the turn of the last century—many still bearing original decoratively painted panels, art deco glass courtyard doors and elevators, and marble stairwells with elaborate period ironwork. It is in the side streets though, where you can see oustanding examples of residential eclectic and art nouveau architecture that survived the war and are lovingly preserved. The examples listed below are near Piazzale Duca d'Aosta in the Crocetta—an unusual trident-shaped, pedestrianized part of the neighborhood, close to the Crocetta market and GAM; and just off Corso Francia, near Piazza Statuto. Note also that via Revel, just south of the Cittadella itself, is also checkered with fine, more traditional art nouveau buildings.

- Villino Mazzuchelli, *via Legnano, 45*
- Palazzina Turbiglio, *Corso Trento, 11*
- Palazzina Belmondo, *Corso Galileo Ferraris, 70*
- Casa Avezzano, *via Vico, 2*
- Casa Fenoglio, *La Fleur, via Principe d'Acaja, 11*
- Casa Tasca, *via Beaumont, 3*
- Villino Raby, *Corso Francia, 8/bis*
- Palazzina Masino, *via Piffetti, 5*

THE MODERN AGE

The architectural character of Turin after World War I is directly linked to change in the political and social climate of the time—war, industrial strife, the rise of Fascism. With the exception of the FIAT Lingotto factory, virtually no building work took place in Turin, in effect suspending architectural expression for close to a decade. Rationalism brewed beneath the surface and with the war still fresh in the memories of Italians, emerged fully fledged around the time of the 1928 expo, a modern tonic to the now seemingly excessive florid art nouveau style. Aiming to design buildings not only of great clarity, but also with the user or resident in mind, attention to function and material were paramount. However, rationalism was never a well-established movement in Turin, and was short-lived in any event, as the Fascist influence took hold of public projects (via Roma is the best example of the overlap between these two moments), soon enough to be replaced by rebuilding efforts after heavy bombardment of the city during the war. A number of pre- and post-war examples of rationalism are notable for their experimentation and for highlighting both the limitations and successes of the era.

Today, the experimental spirit continues, and indeed, is encouraged. Buildings from the city's most prolific period of modern building, between the late 1950s and the mid- to late-Sixties (many built for the Italia '61 expo), are being renovated, repurposed, and celebrated as the modern masterpieces they are.

· Casa dell'Obelisco, *Piazza Crimea, 2*
· Villa Gualino, *viale Settimo Severo, 65*
· Palazzo *della Moda and Torino Esposizioni, Corso Massimo d'Azeglio, 15*

- Fiat Mirafiori, *Corso Giovanni Agnelli, 200*
- Municipal Technical Offices Building, *Piazza San Giovanni, 5*
- Italia '61 Exhibition, *Corso Unità d'Italia, at via Ventimiglia*
- Chamber of Commerce, *via San Francesca da Paola, 24*
- Casa Aurora, *Corso Giulio Cesare, 29*
- Suore della Carità di Santa Giovanna Antida, *via Principessa Felicita di Savoia, 8–12*

WAR AND RESISTANCE

THE SECOND WORLD WAR TOOK A HEAVY TOLL IN TURIN, WHOSE VAST AUTO-motive and electrical industry made it an important military target. Even today, the city can still feel heavily scarred by and still in touch with the war. Severely damaged by British and American bombs—while the Italians fought as part of the Axis powers—it was further devastated by the Germans when Mussolini was forced from office and King Vittorio Emanuele II switched allegiances. The first bomb fell in June 1940 and killed seventeen civilians, the last, in April 1945, destroyed a municipal train station, and by the end of the war, almost half of its buildings were rubble and 1,000 factories had been destroyed.

Those numbers, dramatic as they are, pale in comparison to the human toll, of course. By July 1943, half of Turin's 600,000 residents had fled the city; those that remained endured near-nightly bombing raids, and strict food rationing made daily life difficult at best. In Cesare Pavese's magnificent novel that depicts those years, *The House on the Hill*, the narrator describes the experience of living in the hills just outside of Turin during the bombings:

> *I used to climb [further into the hills] as if I too were fleeing the nightly shock of the air-raid alarms. The roads were swarming with people, poor people who scattered to sleep even in the fields, carrying their mattresses on their bicycles or on their backs, shouting and arguing, obstinate, gullible, and amused...We began to climb, everyone discussing the doomed city, the night, and the terrors to come...I knew that during the night the whole city might go up in flames and all its people be killed.*

In all, more than 2,000 civilians died in Turin during the bombing. Forty years after the war, Primo Levi recalled in *Other People's Trades* how Turin's pavements still held evidence of the air raids:

> *The slabs shattered by the exploding bombs have been replaced, but those which were pierced by incendiary bombs have been left in place. These devices were steel prisms which were dropped blindly with so much impetus as to perforate*

*roofs, attics, and ceilings; some of them falling
on the pavements have neatly perforated the ten
centimetre thick stone like a punch cutter...On
seeing them one recalls the macabre rumors
which circulated in wartime, about pedestrians
who had not been quick enough to take shelter
and had been pierced from head to foot.*

But perhaps most traumatic in the life of the city
were the waning days of the war. Many of Piedmont's Partisans were joined by factory workers,
who took up arms when they were not producing the
machinery of war, and together fiercely struggled
for control of the city with the occupying German
forces. Dozens of small plaques, called *lapide*, dedicated to the partisan dead still line the streets of
Turin, often emblazoned with fresh flowers on anni-
versaries. They are a moving tribute to the heroism of
oridinary Torinesi at an extraordinary time, and one
often sees war veterans at cultural and civic events
in Turin with their regimental pins and banners.

Hundreds of Turin's thriving Jewish community
were deported in the years between 1938, when
Mussolini's race laws went into effect, and 1945,
and few—as Primo Levi's heart-rending books
attest—returned. (One historian estimates only five

per cent returned alive to Italy.) A small memorial to them can be seen near the platform in Porta Nuova, from where they were deported in boxcars. Turin's synagogue, built in 1880, was levelled by a bomb in November 1942, but fully rebuilt and operational by 1949. A poignant photo from the Instituto piemontese per la storia della resistenza of the first service held after the end of the war shows the congregation gathered before the freestanding facade and gates to the synagogue—nothing but rubble visible behind where the doors once were. Today, Turin's Jewish community numbers about 1,000, less than half of what it was before the war.

Compared to other European countries, this part of Italy's wartime experience remains relatively undiscussed. The new Museo diffuso della Resistenza, della Deportazione, della Guerra, dei Diritti, e della Libertà (see page 47) has gone a long way to improve historical understanding. Its basement features an interactive display about Turin and the war, including the deportation of Jews and political radicals, the German occupation, the Partisan movement, and so on. There is a guided tour to an air-raid shelter in a tunnel beneath the building, and its archives are full of oral testimony from contemporary participants and eyewitnesses.

Visitors to the city with an interest in this part of Turin's history will also be especially interested in the last rooms of the Museo del Risorgimento (see page 50), which thoroughly summarizes through documents and ephemera the struggle for the city in the last days of World War II.

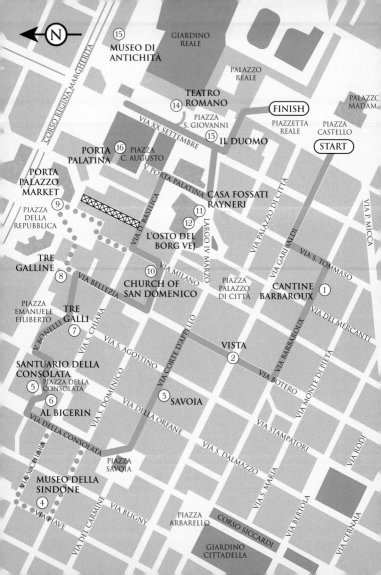

IL QUADRILATERO

*From Piazza Castello to Piazza Savoia
to Piazzetta Reale*

⚜

*A walk through the narrow, cobblestone streets of the city's
Roman quarter, thriving today with cafes, galleries, and
boutiques that have taken up residence in restored palazzos
of centuries past. The walk also includes Porta Palazzo,
Europe's largest food market and the center of Turin's multiethnic community; the remains of the Roman gate to the city,
a Roman theater, and the Museo di Antichità; the Duomo
and the chapel that houses the Holy Shroud; and food and
drink ranging from the oldest cafe in the city to au courant
wine bars.*

1½ TO 2 HOURS WITHOUT STOPS

THE PORTICOED AND PEDESTRIANIZED
PIAZZA CASTELLO (START) WAS THE HEART OF
Savoy Turin and remains at the center of bustling civic life
today. Government offices and the Archivio di Stato, which
occasionally mounts exhibits from its collection here, line
the square. The arcade along the northern edge of the
square is lined with plaques and memorials to war dead,

prominent politicians, and even Erasmus, who attended the nearby University of Turin. Students there have worn off the patina of his pinky finger after decades of rubbing it for good luck before exams. Palazzo Reale (which I discuss in Walk 2) fills the north side, with the elegant royal gardens hidden behind it. The hulking Palazzo Madama dominates the huge square and is a physical timeline of architectural styles. Two smaller towers on the inside of the structure were once the *Porta Pretoria*—the eastern gates to the Roman city. In the early 1300s the red brick structure, best seen from the via Po side, was added to what remained of the Roman complex and, in the first years of the fifteenth century, the forbidding brick towers on the front of the building gave it a fortress-like feel. In 1718, court architect Filippo Juvarra was brought in to raise the standard of the building to that of royal palace for the duke's mother (or *madama reale*), Marie Christine of France. He transformed the western facade of the palace with a classical design and a grand "scissor" staircase in the space of only three years. An imposing 1937 memorial to Duca d'Aosta Emanuele Filiberto is installed on the eastern side of the palazzo; while an antique guidebook claims that the sculpture "disturbs the majesty of the medieval facade," local skateboarders seem to like it just fine and enjoy using the pediment as an ad hoc skate ramp.

With your back to Juvarra's Baroque facade leave the piazza onto via Garibaldi, the oldest street in the city. Once the Roman *decumanus maximus*—its main street—via

Garibaldi is today the longest pedestrian street in Europe. In 1736, an edict was passed to "correct" the street and its wayward shopfronts, and it was soon straightened to its even proportions and regular facades: five handsome floors of residential apartments with shops on the ground, as it remains today. Alas, the majority of the shops along via Garibaldi are chain retailers or local shops aimed strictly at the teen set.

Make the second left, onto via San Tommaso, where Saint Tommaso Break, on the right, offers excellent Ligurian focaccia and pizza by the slice and Libreria Araba Fenice has a good selection of new titles and children's books. Check for notices in the doorways of Galleria Weber and the Paolo Tonin Gallery; both galleries are multi-roomed, former *cortile* apartments, and often have exhibitions worth stopping in for. Just before San Tommaso reaches via Monte di Pietà, near via Pietro Micca, Marta Bera's delightful store is packed with cookies, biscuits, and *grissini*, the traditional breadsticks of Turin. Across the street, her sister runs Bera Bruna *latteria*, where one can enjoy the original mid-century fittings and the proprietess' warmth.

Retrace your footsteps for half a block and make a left onto via Barbaroux, the heart of the Quadrilatero. There are oddball antiques and bijoux shops along the way, and the cheerful Cantine Barbaroux ① makes an excellent stop for lunch or a glass of wine. The cosy interior is cool in the warmer months, but consider sitting outside or near

73

one of the open windows looking onto the street to partake of the congenial atmosphere of the neighborhood. Further along via Barbaroux is the church of San Francesco d'Assisi, with a facade and altar by Vittone, built in 1761. If it is open, look for the Molineri paintings and the wooden sculptures of the patron saint by Plura and Clemente. Further still along via Barbaroux is the Archivio della Città, which often has temporary exhibits from its holdings of Torinese prints, maps, books, and documents; their little shop sells facsimile editions of historic books and prints.

Make a right onto via Botero. There's a nice wine shop, Mille Vigne, just on the right, and the church of Santi Martiri Solutore, Avventore e Ottavio, will be on the left, at the corner with via Garibaldi; built in 1577 in honor of the city's patron saints, to a design by Pellegrino Pellegrini. It has been embellished over the centuries, most notably by the addition of a Juvarra altar in 1734 and a marble floor by Vittone, who also restored the facade in 1768. Crossing via Garibaldi offers a magnificent vista ② on either side: to your right, Palazzo Madama, perfectly aligned at the end of via Garibaldi; to your left—if it's clear out—the Alps. Across via Garibaldi, via Botero becomes via Bellezia; continue on for one block to via Corte d'Appello, and turn left. On the left side of the street is Loràn Camicirie, an old-fashioned shirtmaker, refreshing after the high street buzz of via Garibaldi. Just further along is the Savoia restaurant ③ (see page 125), a good stop if you're doing the walk in the evening, where Mauro Bernardi makes sophisticated

Piedmontese cuisine in an appropriately sophisticated setting (though note you'll likely need a reservation). Straight ahead on the right is Palazzo di Barolo, at the corner of via delle Orfane. One of the best preserved examples of an early seventeenth-century noble residence, the palazzo is now used mainly for cultural events, but is occasionally open to the public. The frescoes, furniture, elaborate stuccowork, and staircase by Baroncelli are worth visiting if it is open. Otherwise continue straight ahead on via Corte d'Appello to Piazza Savoia, where an obelisk raised in 1853 to mark an end to the archaic ecclesiastical court system reads, "The law is the same for everyone." Something of a regional time-capsule was buried under the monument: it contains a bottle of Barbera, a packet of *grissini*, and a copy of *La Gazzetta del Popolo*, the daily paper that led the fund-drive to build the obelisk.

Leave the piazza on the north side, at via della Consolata. (You might want to make a left at via San Domenico to visit the Museo della Sindone ④, which is two blocks away, before returning. There is a film and a guided tour, so this visit may take up to an hour, if not more. Otherwise just continue straight ahead.) One-and-a-half blocks ahead is Piazza Consolata and the Santuario della Consolata ⑤ (dedicated to Maria Consolatrice, Our Lady of Consolation), accessed through the neo-classical doorway to the right. Long considered the city's most beloved church, the building is the 1678 creation of Guarino Guarini. It replaced the many-times-rebuilt Romanesque church of

Sant'Andrea from the tenth century (in fact this spot has been a place of worship since the fifth century). The brick belltower in the small piazza is all that remains of that original structure. Around 1715, Juvarra expanded Guarini's church, adding the central oval portion, the presbytery, and the grand altar flanked by marble angels. This is a deeply moving, eerie place. There is never a time when the devoted aren't visiting: masses are well-subscribed and streams of religious tourists are a regular feature. One of the most remarkable—and modern—features, and what moves me most, are the hundreds of votive paintings offered by locals and the faithful over the years that line the walls of the corridors and rooms to the right of the main chapel. Artistically naïve, these images of personal tragedies, family miseries, and—most of all—wartime sorrows, including many depictions of partisans killed in action or in reprisal (many were done by a single artist whom families hired to visualize their offering), are an overwhelmingly powerful display of the history of war and resistance in Turin, and seeing them is a memorable and strange experience. Around the corner from the church are the remains of a Roman tower, uncovered only in 1885, which marked the northern corner of the old Roman city.

Piazza della Consolata is a fine spot to pass some time and watch ordinary Torinesi go about their day, enjoyable in the warmer months when concerts are sometimes held in front of the church and locals and visitors mix in the square. Its odd shape provides nooks for wine bars and cafes, the most famous being Al Bicerin ⑥. You can hardly fail to be drawn into its tiny space once you peek through the curtains of the city's oldest surviving cafe. Founded in 1763, Al Bicerin was renowned for being one of Count Cavour's regular haunts, and famously serves the drink that gave the cafe its name and which many consider emblematic of Turin: a hot, frothy, concoction of coffee, whipped cream, and chocolate. If that's not to your liking, a coffee at one its tiny marble tables and velvet benches might be. Even though it has become a stop on every tourist itinerary, it still caters to a dedicated local following, too. In nicer weather, Il Bacaro, a friendly Venetian wine bar and restaurant, is ideal for *aperitivi* out on the piazza; they serve a good seafood *fritto misto* and superb Venetian *salumi* and cheese plates. Just beyond, the square turns into a very short block called via Maria Adelaide, which lets out onto via delle Orfane.

Make a left onto via delle Orfane, and then a right onto the winding via Bonelli. This is one of the creative centers of the increasingly hip Quadrilatero. Stop and browse at the art bookstore Gilibert before via Bonelli widens and meets via San'tAgostino, where Tre Galli ⑦ offers a little bit of Parisian-style lounging in the heart of old Turin. Further along via Bonelli are the clothing boutiques Galleria Pia's and Autopsie Vestamentaire, and the ceramics workshop Unomi—all worth some time.

At this point, you may want to make a left at via Bellezia for Tre Galline ⑧, if it's near mealtime. One of the most traditional restaurants in Turin, it offers a fine prixe fixe option. If it's before two (and not a Sunday), you may also want to continue past Tre Galline into the vibrant Porta Palazzo market ⑨ at Piazza della Repubblica. Ignore the cheap handbags and kitchen gadgets and dive into the restored market halls for meat, cheese, and fish—all heady with the perfume of their stock in trade. The new glass building to the left, by Massimiliano Fuksas, holds the recently organized clothing market. While the newly orderly arrangement somewhat sanitizes the experience of Porta Palazzo, it doesn't discourage the thousands of locals who rely on it for their daily shopping.

If you decide to forego the market detour, make a right, walk two blocks to via San Domenico and make a left. The church of San Domenico ⑩ has been rebuilt and transformed since its founding in the early fourteenth century, but was meticulously restored to its original Gothic state between 1906 and 1909. The belltower and masonry vaults inside date from the late fifteenth century. In the late eighteenth century, two aisles at the eastern side of the church were demolished in order for via Milano to be straightened and regraded (to a plan by Juvarra), giving the church its oddly sunken entrance. At the very end of the left-hand aisle, restored portions of the original frescoed ceiling are visible.

Make a left on via Milano and a right on via della Basilica. On the left side is the sadly neglected Galleria Umberto I—perhaps the regeneration of the area around the market will resurrect it to its former glory. Just past the next corner is the slick AB+ restaurant and club, housed in a restored medieval palazzo; up on the left is a plaque dedicated to Renaissance poet Torquato Tasso, who lived in the building in 1578. This house, one of the oldest residences still standing in Turin, was renovated by Carlo di Castellamonte in the early seventeenth century. For all the care taken in lovingly preserving buildings of note here, it may come as a surprise that the long, low-slung building visible across the way was recently the subject of a heated conservation debate. There are people in Turin who love this 1960s municipal building. Unfortunately, it disrupts a view that encompasses Roman and Baroque Turin that may have been recaptured on the completion of the archeological park. Alas, the building is staying and has been "restored."

Continue along and Porta Palatina will appear to your left; around the corner to your right will be Largo IV Marzo. The building on the corner is Casa Fossati Rayneri ⑪, it dates from the fourteenth century and is one of the few surviving medieval private houses in Turin. On the ground floor wrapping the corner are modern antique shop Galleria Cristiani, the quaint Bottego IV Marzo, and L'osto del Borg Vej ⑫, an excellent lunch or dinner choice.

Continue along the Largo IV Marzo towards Piazza San Giovanni and the Cattedrale di San Giovanni, commonly known as the Duomo ⑬. This vantage point offers a clear view of Guarini's fantastic spiral dome for the Cappella della Santa Sindone, under restoration since a devastating fire in 1997. The Duomo, opened in 1498, is a modest Renaissance cathedral, squat and even ill-proportioned. Still, if it's not an example of great architecture, it is a stylistic exception in Turin, where the Renaissance only paused and the Gothic barrelled without hesitation into the Baroque (the wooden doors of the Duomo, in fact, were carved by Turin's master Baroque woodworker, Carlo Maria Ugliengo). The cathedral itself was designed by Amedeo del Caprina da Settignano, a Tuscan architect who modelled it on the work of Brunelleschi and Alberti. Not nearly as well-executed as the work that inspired it, its facade is still pleasing and the pixellated tone of the marble suits Turin's more somber (and less exultant Renaissance) mood. Inside, the sobriety continues: the nave is lightly decorated in comparison to its Baroque neighbors—including the one right next door. Visible at the end of the main aisle is the Cappella della Sacra Sindone, its dramatic jet-black Frabosa marble portal at the time of writing masked by the mediocre trompe l'oeil installed after the 1997 fire. Intended as a shrine to hold the casket containing the Holy Shroud, the chapel is shoehorned between the Duomo and the western wing of the Palazzo Reale, epitomizing the Savoys' combined religious and civic rule. Work on the chapel began in 1611 by Carlo di Castellamonte to a Vitozzi design, was abandoned due to the outbreak of war and resumed in 1656 by Bernardo Quadri, only to be halted again within a few years. In 1668, Guarino Guarini, who was then working on the nearby church of San Lorenzo, was called on to complete the design. Guarini faced a huge challenge: not only to build on a half-finished structure, but also to satisfy the eccentric demands of the Savoys that the chapel be accessible from the Palazzo Reale, that it be connected to the cathedral by a staircase, and that it be a grand architectural statement as significant as the relic it was designed to contain. But Guarini succeeded splendidly. His sixty-meter, drum-shaped dome was completed in 1694, ten years after his death, and it's his crowning achievement—and the chapel's. The hexagonal structure appears almost woven, and the interlaced windows as it winds upward give the exterior cupola a spiralling beehive effect. Inside the circular chapel there is a stunning central altar by Bertola, beneath which the black marble of the portal extends to the floor. Bertola and Borelli's elaborate casket containing the Shroud itself—four layers thick, seven locks—is on view, behind glass, at the back of the Duomo.

Beside the Duomo in Piazza San Giovanni there is a belltower built in 1470 (with a belfry added by Juvarra in 1722). But just past it, at the northern corner of the piazza, are the ruins of the Teatro Romano ⑭, which were excavated in 1899 during construction of a new wing to the Palazzo Reale. Datable to the first century, it is said to have occupied an entire block and incorporated all the traits of a classical theater, traces of which are still visible: the *cavea*, or stepped seating, the orchestra for the *chorum*, and the *pulpitum*, where the performances were staged. It may even have had a wooden roof. After 69 AD, owing to a population surge, the building was enlarged and, mirroring the fortunes of the robust Roman city, lined in marble.

Further north along via XX Settembre is the underrated Museo di Antichità ⑮, carved out of the Palazzo Reale's *orangerie*. It has an impressive collection of relics from the days of *Augusta Taurinorum* amassed during extensive excavations around Piedmont during the eighteenth and nineteenth centuries. These finds were added to the collection, begun in the sixteenth century by Emanuele Filiberto, of flawless Etruscan pieces. A clever architectural extension of the lower floors into the former gardens of the palazzo will soon house a gallery dedicated to the history of the city of Turin.

To the left of the museum is the best-preserved Roman relic in the city, Porta Palatina ⑯ —the northern gate of *Augusta Taurinorum*. Built in the first century BC, the two towers are about one hundred feet high and sixteen-sided, and served less as a means of defense than as a proud emblem of the city's political station. Of the four arched openings in the base, the two wider ones were reserved for wheeled traffic (not just chariots—photos from before the Second World War, two thousand years after the gate was built, show cars driving through it) and the two smaller ones for pedestrians. Grooves that facilitated the lowering and raising of portcullises are still visible on the inside of the arches. Remnants of a paved courtyard are barely visible beneath the arches and through the weeds. Porta

Palatina wasn't always "merely" a historical ruin. After architect Antonio Bertola convinced Vittorio Amedeo II not to demolish it (!), it was used as a prison for the vicarage and even until the late eighteenth century it was used as a women's prison. It was damaged during the war, and, somewhat isolated and ignored for years, will soon be the centerpiece of an "archaeological park" incorporating the gate into an ambitious green space, once again accessible to the public. The statues of Julius Caesar and Caesar Augustus on the southern side of the gate are modern copies installed during the Fascist era—a testament to Mussolini's Caesar fixation.

From here, you can return to the adjoining Piazzetta Reale and Castello (**FINISH**) via the covered alleyway behind Piazza San Giovanni where Walk 2, Il Centro, begins.

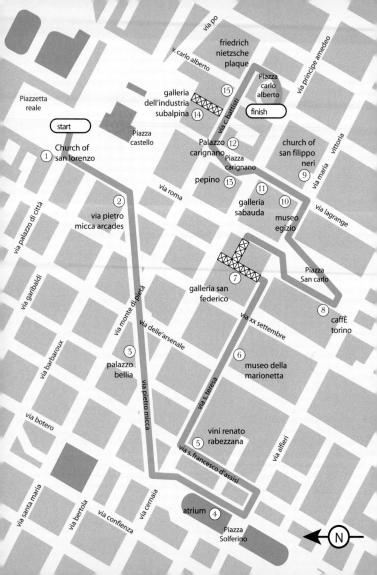

IL CENTRO

From Piazza Castello to Piazza San Carlo
to Piazza Carlo Alberto

❧

The Baroque heart of Turin is bustling with everyday activity
and some of the finest cultural treasures in the country. Visit
a bookshop that is also one of the most popular cafes in town
and have a coffee in Turin's "living room" before feasting
your eyes on the treasures at the Museo Egizio and Galleria
Sabauda. È

1½ TO 2 HOURS WITHOUT STOPS

O N THE NORTH SIDE OF THE ENORMOUS PIAZZA CASTELLO IS PALAZZO REALE (START), the official royal palace of the Savoy family from the middle of the seventeenth century until 1865. The only original structural element left to the exterior is Amedeo di Castellamonte's (son of Savoy court architect Carlo di Castellamonte) facade of 1658; since then the building has undergone almost constant renovation. Behind the palace lies the Giardini Reale, the romantic, tree-filled royal gardens, designed by André Le Nôtre, the architect of the gardens at Versailles. While neither as big nor as grand as

Versailles, the recently replanted Giardini Reale is peaceful and lovingly manicured, and it is visitable for a small fee. The luxuriously furnished royal apartments of Palazzo Reale may also be visited by guided tour (in Italian only), if you've not already had your fill of Baroque interiors elsewhere. At the eastern end of Piazza Castello is the Teatro Regio, Carlo Mollino's celebrated undulating 1973 design that replaced an original Benedetto Alfieri theater from 1740, which was destroyed by fire in 1936. Plans to rebuild were delayed by war and then the premature death of the first architect called upon to carry out the new project. Carlo Mollino was given the commission in 1965 and designed a state of the art auditorium (which later had to be acoustically upgraded, anyway) and a lipstick-red lobby. Tours can be taken when there are no afternoon performances; call or visit the theater for details.

In contrast, directly across the piazza is Guarino Guarini's 1666 church of San Lorenzo ①. The exterior was never completed to plan, hence the flat, almost residential facade beneath the cupola that adjoins the Palazzo Reale and blends seamlessly with the square. The church was administered by the Theatine Order, of which—interestingly—Guarini was a priest. The dome here is the real draw—resting on great arches and eight windows that illuminate the entire nave, San Lorenzo is a tribute to verticality and a triumph for such a narrow plot of land.

Leave the piazza on the open end and make a right onto the arcaded via Pietro Micca. Here begins a grand stretch of the arcades ② that have made Turin justly famous. The sixteenth-century architect and urban planner, Ascanio Vitozzi, was responsible for some of the first arcades in the Palazzo Castello. Originally planned to allow the Savoys a sheltered passage between various royal establishments, they spread over time to many of the main thoroughfares throughout the city, and have become one of Turin's most widely recognized features. On this side of the piazza, rising above the corner of via Pietro Micca, is the twenty-one storey Torre Littoria, designed by Armando Melis de Villa and completed in 1933. At the time, its disruption to the uniformity of the city was a shock—as much for its ugliness as its height, and for years it was known as *l'obrobrio*, or "the disgrace." Though not strictly a result of Fascist building reform, the Torre Littoria evinces some of the will towards monumental scale of the time, but with a light, almost nautical sense.

Turn right under the arcades of via Pietro Micca. Initially, if unoriginally, called via Diagonale, it broke Turin's rigid street grid and was the key element of a massive slum clearance plan that began in 1885. Palazzo Bellia ③, on the right side at number 4–8, is the 1894 work of architect Carlo Ceppi, the father of what has been called "Torinese eclecticism." (He was also responsible for the decorative work on the exterior of Porta Nuova station.) The bow windows topped by mini-towers were made possible by an innovative, early use of reinforced concrete.

Continue along via Pietro Micca's tiled sidewalk. On the

right is the overwrought but loved Caffè Norman, with its chandeliers and towers of *tramezzini* and *stuzzechini*, and further still the excellent La Torre de Abele bookshop. Just ahead and hard to miss, the florid gable and St. Mark's lion of the 1909 Assicurazioni Generali Venezia building give Turin an unexpected touch of Venice.

Make a left into Piazza Solferino, until the early nineteenth century the site of the city's wood, straw, and hay market. Today, the Atrium ④ is the centerpoint of this otherwise unremarkable—and rectangular—square, bordered by traffic and parking lanes. The Atrium is a two-part tourism office: the AtriumCittà and the Atrium2006 offer elaborate overviews of Turin's wide ranging urban plans (revolving around, unsurprisingly, cars and transport) and the winter Olympic games. However, there are two thoughtful films of the city "then to now," and lots of maps, models, and plans to peruse. Across the piazza is Teatro Alfieri, its classical motifs and capital unusual in this eclectic neighborhood; after nearly 150 years, it still hosts an impressive roster of plays.

With your back to the theater, leave the square at via Alfieri and, after one block, make a left onto via San Francesco d'Assisi. In Roman Turin this street was the *cardo maximus*, the north–south artery that—combined with present-day via Garibaldi—defined the shape of the ancient city. Today, a sweet collection of small shops lines both sides of the quiet street. Simona Bruno makes men's and women's shirts to order; Fitzcarraldo sells small antiques and bijoux jewelery;

and Magic Lantern has a selection of antique Italian jewelery and small silver pieces. Across the street is Il Granaio, which makes its own pasta, and also supplies the attached cafeteria-style restaurant, Caffè 27, which is always busy at lunchtime with local office workers. Plates of fresh pasta, prosciutto and melon, and a choice of two or three second courses are surprisingly satisfying and make a quick, easy lunch stop. Up the street is Vini Renato Rabezzana ⑤, established in Turin in 1913 and presided over by Carlo Rabezzana, the founder's grandson, who sells the family's own organically produced wine in addition to the finest of Piedmontese labels.

When you reach the corner of via Santa Teresa, the somewhat underwhelming Porta Susa—soon to take over from Porta Nuova as the main terminus for international trains—is to the left with the Alps beyond it, while in the distance to the right are the hills rising up above the Po. Turn toward the hills along via Santa Teresa. On the right is the church of Santa Teresa, built between 1642 and 1647. Wartime bombing of the neighborhood has marooned the church with only part of what was once a formal square out front. It is the Juvarra altar in the chapel to San Giuseppe, from 1733, that makes visiting it worthwhile. An unpromising doorway to the right of the church is the entrance to the delightful Museo della Marionetta ⑥ (also home to the Teatro Gianduja and Cinema Kong), the Lupi family's 5,000-piece collection of marionettes, costumes, stage sets, and ephemera from the troupe's past. An appointment is required (see page 43) but you might try knocking anyway if you're without one—friendly souls there have been known to open their doors even for the unprepared. Once you descend the dark stairwell and the lights are flipped on, you are left to yourself to browse the rooms of cases displaying the history—in puppets—of the Lupi family's troupe. Occasional marionette performances still occur and are affordable and wildly popular. Further along Santa Teresa is the Galleria San Federico ⑦, one of Turin's most beautiful covered passages. Originally commissioned by the Agnelli family in 1931 to house new offices for their newspaper *La Stampa*, Galleria San Federico was part of a city-wide attempt to restore the neo-Baroque style through new building projects, though you might not guess it from the high-art deco glass block in the ceiling vaults. It has seen better days, and many of the shops inside are shuttered. The sumptuously art deco Lux Cinema has valiantly fought closure, but screens mainly dubbed American block-busters, alas.

In the gallery, turn right at the Lux and exit onto via Roma. Turn right to enter Piazza San Carlo—often called Turin's "living room," but really the hub that connects old Turin to new. Built on the site of a Roman amphithe-ater—as the centerpiece of the city and the masterwork of Carlo di Castellamonte—the piazza was conceived in 1620, begun in 1637, and finally completed nearly twenty years later. It was the main public space during the city's seven-teenth-century southern expansion and embraced the roles of marketplace (for wheat and rice), military parade, and meeting place—not so unlike today. The rigid uniformity of the facades around the piazza was an attempt to detract from visual signs of property ownership, even though it was still occupied almost exclusively by the nobility. Severe damage to the piazza during World War II required near total reconstruction that lasted through the 1950s, but at number 183 there are some visible remains of the eighteenth-century Palazzo Solaro del Borgo. The columns supporting the arcades today were once double marble pillars topped by glass oculi—some are still visible in the arcades along the south side of the piazza. They were subsequently transformed into large pillars (for strength) and the decorative glass was replaced with ornamental stucco panels.

The historic center of Turin's cafe society, the porticoes of San Carlo conceal two of the city's most famous spots: the Caffè San Carlo and the Caffè Torino ⑧. Both are equally over the top in gilt decor and tuxedoed service (and overpriced coffee), and the San Carlo—founded in 1822—is among the oldest in the city. Caffè Torino is said to have been one of Cesare Pavese's favorite places, and I prefer it to San Carlo as a small tribute to him. The arcades of the piazza are now lined with shops, including the curious (and famously unfriendly) food importer P.A.I.S.S.A. and various banks and clothiers. Soon, when restoration work on the piazza is complete, a World War II-era bomb shelter will be visible in the underground car park. Standing sentry in the middle of the piazza is the equestrian statue of Emanuele Filiberto sheathing his sword at the end of the Battle of San Quintino, in 1557, by Carlo Marochetti, the Turin-born sculptor later famous for his work in England, particularly his contributions to the Albert Memorial in Hyde Park and the Albert and Victoria tomb in Frogmore. His Filiberto (also called the *Neuv Caval d'Brons*, from which a swanky restaurant in the piazza takes its name) was unveiled in 1838, and was intended to be surrounded by an elaborate series of fountains and other statuary. It was displayed to some acclaim at the Louvre before being installed in the piazza. Beyond it, at the southern end of the piazza, are the "twin churches" of Santa Cristina (left) and San Carlo (right). It is a mystery who is responsible for the design of San Carlo, built in 1619; it has been attributed to Carlo di Castellamonte, Andrea Costaguta, Maurizio Valperga, and Galleani di Ventimiglia. Santa Cristina was designed in 1639 by Castellamonte, shortly before his death, and on the site of what was formerly his own home. The facade was designed much later, around 1715, by Juvarra—one of his earliest commissions in Turin.

Piazza San Carlo bisects the wide via Roma, and the street's lower half, including Porta Nuova, is visible from here. It was redesigned between 1931–37, and while the project was not strictly directed by the regime (planning for it began in 1920), the flat, severe Fascist influence is obvious. It was the biggest urban planning initiative after the cutting of via Pietro Micca fifty years earlier. The northern half of via Roma, that towards Piazza Castello, is still firmly rooted in the Baroque. In either style, via Roma is the main artery of the Centro and joining the Torinesi on their traditional stroll, or *passeggiata*, after lunch on Sunday to chat, to window-shop, and to eat *gelati* under its porticoes is a pleasure not to be missed. You may even be lucky enough to find yourself in Turin on one of its occasional "car free" Sundays, when via Roma (among other major streets) becomes a grand thoroughfare and pedestrians flood the street.

Leave the piazza by making a right onto via Maria Vittoria. The old shopfront of Steffanone, one of the finest purveyors of *salumi* in the city, is on the right. If you fancy a picnic lunch later, this is a good stop for provisions—Steffanone carries everything you'll need from meats and cheeses to bread and wine. Ahead, on the left, is the church of San Filippo Neri ⑨, another masterpiece of Baroque church architecture by Juvarra. It is Turin's largest church, and probably my favorite. Juvarra worked on it for nearly fifteen years once he took over the project from Antonio Bettino, whose flawed design caused the dome of the structure to collapse; rebuilding finally began in 1730. There even exists a Guarino Guarini drawing for this church, dating to before Bettino's attempt, a design that never got further than a sketch. The neo-classical facade, an unusual addition to what is otherwise a typically Baroque brick construction, was added only in 1891 (to Juvarra's original design). Inside, the single space is awash with natural light from windows surrounding the nave and in the side chapels. An enormous antique floral rug rests on the modest wooden plank floor at the entrance in stark contrast to Juvarra's elaborate marble columns on the altar. Next door, the oratory, built in the 1860s, is used for lectures and art events, and will soon house a new museum of applied arts. Visible above the courtyard in front of the church, there is—curiously—a cannonball that lodged in the wall of the building next door on May 20, 1799, during the French siege of the city (there is a similar sight at Consolata, too).

From the front of San Filippo Neri, make a right onto via Lagrange, towards the hulking Collegio dei Nobili, home to two magnificent museums, the Museo Egizio ⑩ and Galleria Sabauda ⑪. The design of the building has long been attributed to Guarino Guarini, and some details are reminiscent of the neighboring Palazzo Carignano, but it was designed by Michelangelo Garove. After more than twenty years of construction, beginning in 1679, only half the building was completed. Today, the two museums share the mammoth space quite comfortably, which is undergoing improvements to give the Egyptian collection some breathing room. These two museums are Turin institutions and their vast collections are national treasures. The Sabauda is an extremely tranquil place, where the atmosphere borders on devotional. While you may vie for space with schoolchildren and tour groups at the Museo Egizio, the collection should absolutely not be missed.

Continue straight on via Lagrange into Piazza Carignano, the most pleasing spot in the city and the place I always visit first when I arrive. It is an odd space, a square only in the loose sense of the word, longer than it is wide. At the center there is a statue of Vinenzo Gioberti, a liberal priest who participated in the Risorgimento (and published a book called *The Moral and Civil Preeminence of the Italians*; needless to say, long out of print...) and was exiled to France for his efforts; he returned to Turin—to great fanfare—in 1848. The Teatro Carignano, on the west side of the piazza, stages important national productions and is next door to Ristorante Il Cambio, the luxurious dining choice of aristocrats for nearly two centuries. Still popular, its plush interior sits shrouded behind curtains. Palazzo Carignano ⑫, perhaps Guarini's masterpiece, dominates the scene. I can look at its brick and terracotta decorations and its undulating form for hours. I can also happily watch as groups of tourists stare agog at it—pleased that nearly everyone finds some wonder in it, as well. Begun in 1679 for the Savoy duke Emanuele Filiberto (who, incidentally, was deaf and mute), on land that was formerly his father's stables, the building somehow manages to seem pure Baroque and modern at the same time. A propeller-like motif runs up and down the facade, the wings—built to accommodate the interior oval form of the building—seem bursting at the seams. The main-floor windows are decorated with friezes portraying a Native American headdress commemorating a French victory over the Iroquois in Canada, a campaign the Duke financed. From this vantage point, you can also see the back of San Filippo Neri and get a sense of Juvarra's sophisticated brickwork—otherwise disguised by the church's classical facade. But my favorite thing in the piazza is simpler. Behind the statue of Gioberti is the window for Pepino **⓭**, which originated the popular *pinguino* (vanilla ice cream on a stick, coated in chocolate) in 1937, and today serves the best gelato in the city. If you're not in the mood for gelato, or have already had your fill, Mood Libri e Caffè, around the left hand side of the piazza, is as good a spot for book browsing as it is for coffee or *aperitivi*; if the weather is good, try to grab a table outside and watch the crowds strolling in from via Roma. Parola, a wine shop and *enoteca* practically next door, is a smart choice for a quieter glass of wine. The bookstore Luxembourg anchors the northeast corner of the piazza at via Accademia delle Scienze. Aside from its excellent selection of Italian books, its English language books on the second floor (and the Sunday *New York Times*), have kept me a little closer to home on longer stays in Turin.

Continue along this pedestrianized bit of via Cesare Battisti to the entrance of the beautiful Galleria dell'Industria Subalpina **⓮**. The glass covered arcade linking Piazza Carlo Alberto and Piazza Castello was designed by Pietro Carrera in 1873. The airy landscaped room holds offices on the second floor and a selection of book and print shops (notably La Casa del Libro), cafes (including the minuscule Bar Mulassano, which opened in 1909 and still retains the feel of that silvery age), and a cinema (which Carrera imagined as an ale-house) below. Further along, at the corner with via Carlo Alberto is a plaque ⑮ marking Friedrich Nietzsche's home in Turin in 1888–89. He boarded with Davide Fino, who ran a bookstall in Piazza Carlo Alberto, and his family at via Carlo Alberto, 6. After years of rootlessness, acute depression, and headaches, Turin was a salve. In a letter to Henrich Koselitz, who had suggested a sojourn in Turin to him, Nietzsche wrote: "Your heart told you what to advise me! This is really the town I can use now! Just the sort of place I can get a hold of and it was like that almost from the first moment…". It was here that he had his miraculous year, writing five of his greatest books including *The Anti-Christ*, some of his well-known work on Wagner, and *Ecce Homo*, which he completed just before going mad in January 1889 (most likely from the effects of syphilis), a condition he dramatically enacted when he lovingly embraced a horse in the street and subsequently lost consciousness. He left for Basel soon after, and died ten years later in Weimar, under his sister's care.

Continue straight for half a block; Piazza Carlo Alberto (FINISH) will appear on your right. Walk 3: Borgo Nuovo, begins here among the majesty of the Biblioteca Nazionale and Palazzo Carignano.

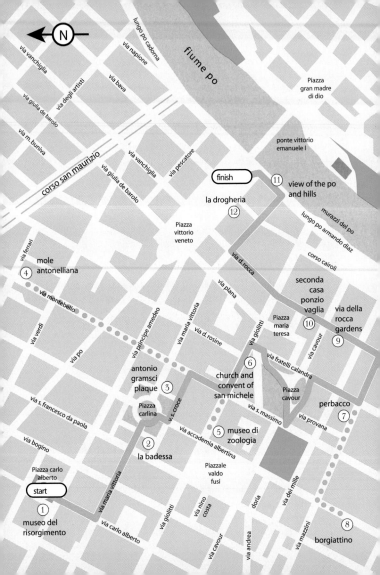

N

via vanchiglia
lungo po cadorna
via napione
via bava
via degli artisti
via giulia de barolo
via m. buniva

fiume po

Piazza
gran madre
di dio

corso san maurizio
via vanchiglia
via giulia de barolo
via pescatore

ponte vittorio
emanuele I

finish

11 view of the po
and hills

la drogheria
12

murazzi del po
lungo po armando diaz

corso cairoli

Piazza
vittorio
veneto

via d. rocca

seconda
casa
ponzio
vaglia
10

via della
rocca
gardens
9

via ferrari

mole
antonelliana
4

via montebello

via verdi
via po
via principe amedeo
via maria vittoria
via plana
via d. rosine

via giolitti
Piazza
maria
teresa

via cavour

via fratelli calandra

antonio
gramsci
plaque
3

Piazza
carlina

via s. croce

6

church and
convent of
san michele

Piazza
cavour

perbacco
7

via provana

via s. francesco da paola

via bogino

2

la badessa

via accademia albertina

5 museo di
zoologia

via s. massimo

Piazza
carlo
alberto

start
1

museo del
risorgimento

via maria vittoria
via carlo alberto

via giolitti

Piazzale
valdo
fusi

via nino
costa

via andrea
doria
via cavour

via dei mille

via mazzini

8

borgiattino

IL BORGO NUOVO

*From Piazza Carlo Alberto to Piazza Carlina
to Piazza Vittorio Veneto*

❖

*This walk is on the short side and a bit further from the most
touristed part of the city, but it takes in some of my favorite
areas. It has great examples of the city's Baroque architecture; the extraordinary Museo del Risorgimento and eerie
zoology museum; regional antique stores and art galleries;
wonderful residential architecture; and delightful places to
eat. The walk ends with a glorious view of the river Po and
surrounding hills and abundant options for a meal or a drink
in Piazza Vittorio Veneto.*

1 TO 1½ HOURS WITHOUT STOPS

BEGIN IN PIAZZA CARLO ALBERTO (START),
AT THE BACK OF THE PALAZZO CARIGNANO.
Between 1860–1865, the palazzo expanded into its gardens to accommodate a parliamentary chamber befitting
the new Italian capital. As it happened, it was never used,
as the capital was transferred from Turin to Florence in
1864 (and finally to Rome in 1870). The extension was
given—in keeping with tastes at the time—a neo-clas-

99

sical facade onto what became Piazza Carlo Alberto. The broad and sunny piazza is closed on the eastern edge by the regal Biblioteca Nazionale, its copper pediment, cartouches, and decorative suits of armour recently restored. Sadly, the interior doesn't live up to the grand facade, but do check to see if an exhibit from the collection is on view—they only happen occasionally, but are typically very good.

On this side of the Palazzo Carignano is the entrance to the Museo del Risorgimento ①, a sprawling museum that chronicles Italy's path to nationhood, as well as some of its experience in the decades since. A museum to the Italian Risorgimento has long existed in Turin (the collection was once held in a space at the Mole Antonelliana, in fact), and there are similar collections in other Italian cities, but it seems appropriate that the most thorough public dissemination of the Risorgimento is held in the rooms of one of the city's grandest palaces, which itself played a role in Italy's first days as a unified nation. It was in Palazzo Carignano's oval chamber that patriots from all over Italy gathered to participate in Italy's first parliament in 1861. The chamber is still intact and on view as part of the museum; there is even a chart showing where each representative sat. The exhibit is quite large, so prepare to spend at least an hour-and-a-half if you decide to go in.

Facing the library, continue right onto via Carlo Alberto. At the corner of via Maria Vittoria is the provincial headquarters for Piedmont, located in the Palazzo dal Pozzo della Cisterna. This was the birthplace of Maria Vittoria, the wife of the first Duke of Aosta; among their many titles, they were even briefly King and Queen of Spain. From via Carlo Alberto, the alert viewer can catch a glimpse through the courtyard of the gorgeous garden—not open to the public, unfortunately—by Henri Duparc, who designed the gardens at Venaria Reale. A waving canopy of colorful provincial flags decorates via Maria Teresa, a street lined with antiques shops, art galleries, and boutiques. Luigi Caretto carries eighteenth- and nineteenth-century pieces, while Galleria Christiani specializes in modern pieces. Kristina Ti, on the righthand side, is a particular favorite of mine: a light and airy boutique that specializes in silky frocks and tiny sweaters.

Straight ahead is Piazza Carlina. Officially known as Piazza Carlo Emanuele II, its nickname was a smirking reference to the Duke's alleged homosexuality, and one that stuck. Dominated by an uninspired monument to Cavour by Giovanni Dupré, Piazza Carlina should have been grandly planned by Amedeo di Castellamonte, but when Carlo Emanuele II died, the square became the city's wine market and later, when the French revolutionary government presided, the site of its guillotine. Later still, privately-owned houses and a variety of buildings hosting religious and charitable organizations began to be built, giving the piazza its dishevelled appearance, unusual for Turin. Today, the pleasingly shabby piazza features bohemian cafes and restaurants, the tram rumbling through, and, like any burgeoning hipster spot, a high-end clothing store or two, as well as the remaining church and converted *palazzi*. The popular Societé Lutece—a good lunch or aperitif stop—anchors one corner of the western side, while La Badessa ②, a restaurant specializing in "monastery cooking," and the art bookshop Agorà, anchor the other. The church of Santa Croce (an addition to a late seventeenth-century cloister) is a Juvarra work of 1718–1730; the stepped belltower steeple was added in the mid-eighteenth century and the facade in 1898. The building has been used during more than one conflict as a military barracks and hospital. At number 15, the magnificent Palazzo dell'Albergo di Virtù, marked by a plaque ③, was home to Antonio Gramsci between 1919–1921, when he was working on *L'Ordine Nuovo* and organizing urban factory workers and countryside farmhands. Though its architect is forgotten, the palazzo (now divided into forty-two apartments) is quite elegant. Most of what is visible dates from the nineteenth century, but it has been built around the foundations of an eighteenth-century house of charity. Its ironic fate is only a few years off, as current plans call for it to be transformed into a luxury hotel. Across the way is the Palazzo Roero di Guarene, with a facade by Juvarra. Vittone's austere Collegio delle Province—set up by King Vittorio Amedeo II to wrest control of education in the city away from the Jesuits—is now home to the Carabinieri.

Leave the square at via Santa Croce. You'll be facing the church of San Pelagia on via San Massimo, built to a design by Filippo di Robilant between 1769–1772. Taking a page from Guarini's book, the wavy asymmetry of the mass of the church is at odds with the ochre paint, classical columns, and pediment facade. Looking left from here, there is a dramatic view of the Mole Antonelliana ④. (You may wish to go visit its spire-high observation deck, with a panoramic view of the city—and its highly recommended cinema museum—now; it's less than a ten-minute walk from here.) Next, make a right onto via San Massimo. At the corner of via Giolitti is the Museo Storico di Zoologia ⑤ and the Museo Regionale di Scienze Naturali (the entrance is to the right on via Giolitti and the recommended zoology museum doesn't require a long visit). A left onto Giolitti reveals the neighborhood's origins as the woodworking district; the street still boasts a concentration of antique dealers, furniture restorers, woodworkers, and other craftspeople. The Church and Convent of San Michele ⑥ at the corner of Giolitti and Piazza Cavour is a beautiful Pietro Bonvicini design in what was once the velvet-making district. Badly bomb-damaged in 1942, restoration efforts have retained the modest brick structure and repaired the illuminating drum dome that gives the interior a fuzzy, otherworldly haze. It is now a Greek Byzantine Catholic church, and small gold-flecked icons decorate the simple single space inside.

Walk diagonally through the wedge of Piazza Cavour, its odd shape and hill the result of being planned around and on the old city walls and battlements. At via San Massimo, you will reach the edge of a another green space, the

Aiuola Balbo, a park of monuments in the Parisian style. Notably there is one of Hungarian political hero and patriot Lajos Kossuth, who was forced into exile for his support of Hungarian independence from Austria and for his writings opposing the Hapsburgs. He settled in Turin in 1859 after many years of rootless exile and lived nearby at via dei Mille, 22. When the Aiuola Balbo was opened in 1835, it was known as the Giardino dei Ripari (a reference to the *ripari*, or shelters, that stood here as part of the city's fortifications), and was constructed as something of an elevated walkway linking neighborhoods. At its center was the high society Rotunda, a cafe preserved only in prints and books. This marks the true start of the Borgo Nuovo—the "new neighborhood," that is, that King Carlo Alberto planned from around 1834 as part of the eastward expansion of the city, towards the river. The emerging upper middle class that sprung from the success of the Risorgimento found the isolated neighborhood of large plots particularly attractive; this was a neighborhood of consuls and professionals that took on something of a suburban tone with the building of large villas and gardens to match. With growth, and befitting its moment as a capital city, the neo-classical style firmly took hold in the Borgo Nuovo. Unusual for Turin at the time, today it drifts seamlessly into the Baroque slightly to the west, and there is a quiet atmosphere of fallen aristocracy in the air.

Leave the piazza at the southeast corner onto via Fratelli Calandra, where at the corner with via dei Mille, you might want to stop for a simple lunch at Al Refettorio. Otherwise, continue on another block and make a left at via Mazzini, where numerous pasta shops, butchers, greengrocers, and chocolatiers make it a kind of gourmet row. (You may want to visit some of them, to the right, before returning this way. Note, too, that there are two especially fine restaurants within two blocks of here: L'agrifolio and my favorite, Perbacco ⑦. In addition, the wonderful cheese shop, Roberto Borgiattino ⑧ is on via della Accademia Albertina.)

After going one block on via Mazzini, turn left at via della Rocca, which runs parallel to the river a couple of blocks away; it's a quiet, old-money shopping and gallery street at the heart of this stately neighborhood. On the right is a surprisingly good sushi restaurant called Kiki, and a few doors down is the eyeglass atelier Baricole, which features frames by Turin-based and other Italian designers. Further along still is the treasure-trove of china Varese Antichità, Peola gallery, and some of the Borgo Nuovo's handsome homes—via della Rocca, cut in 1825, was often referred to by locals as Strada dei Nobili, but its real name derives from the nearby site of a medieval fortress known as La Rocca. Over the years, many of the grand, recessed gardens were reclaimed in order to build multi-family dwellings that replaced or surrounded the owner's home, but few remain today (those that do are via della Rocca 5–15, 20–22, and 27–33, though not all are clearly visible from the street, where gates usually block the view) ⑨.

On the next block of via della Rocca there are two examples of residential architecture by Alessandro Antonelli, who designed the Mole. The Seconda Casa Ponzio Vaglia ⑩ at number 12 is an early example of rental housing; built in 1845, it is almost perfectly intact. Antonelli ardently professed that the provision of rental housing was key to balanced civic and economic life. Casa Ponzio Vaglia at number 14 was built five years earlier and was Antonelli's first apartment building, but it is not as close to its original condition as its neighbor, and has an added upper floor and many later embellishments to the facade.

Soon, on the left side of the street will be Piazza Maria Teresa, a pleasant, shade-dappled park frequented by dog-walkers, students, and those out for a lunchtime stroll. Guglielmo Pepe, on the east side of the piazza, serves a nice lunch (under umbrellas on the piazza itself in good weather).

Borgo Nuovo is full of small art galleries. You may want to see what's on exhibit at the highly regarded Galleria Giampietro Biasutti, for example, before continuing along via della Rocca and making a right onto via Maria Vittoria, where after two short blocks you will reach the river Po. From here there is an astonishing, uninterrupted view ⑪ of all the Collina landmarks (from right to left): Monte dei Capuccini, Gran Madre di Dio, the Ponte Vittorio Emanuele, and off into the distance on the far left, the Basilica di Superga. Just below you are the famed *murazzi*, where bars and clubs have been carved out of the arches beneath the road and fill to overflowing on weekends with revelers.

Make a left on the riverside Lungo Po Armando Diaz and walk into the bottom of Piazza Vittorio Veneto (changed in 1918 from Piazza Vittorio Emanuele I and now more commonly known simply as Piazza Vittorio). The piazza, originally built as a parade grounds and more recently known for its prime parking, is lined with perfectly aligned buildings over an uninterrupted series of porticoes. Monumental in scope, it was planned in the early nineteenth century by Giuseppe Frizzi, who brilliantly negotiated a thirty-six foot drop in the street level from the top of the piazza to the river by progressively lowering the heights of the buildings—a virtually invisible solution. It remains one of the largest *piazze* in Europe. It took years to come about as differences between the king, the mayor's office, the builders, and emerging private land developers vied for space and planning approval. Frizzi's architectural unity and his vision for a modern gateway to the city prevailed and the piazza has been the symbolic center of Turin ever since. On May 6, 1945, thousands of Torinesi crowded into it to celebrate the end of the war and to watch a parade of the Partisans who had liberated their city. You might end the walk with a drink in La Drogheria's ⑫ cosy upstairs mezzanine for two; a coffee at the classic Caffè Elena; or dinner at Porta di Savona. FINISH

CAFES & BARS

CAFES ARE INSEPARABLE FROM THE
FABRIC OF DAILY LIFE IN ITALY AND
nowhere is this more apparent than in Turin, where cafe
society has a long history — often intertwined with literature and politics. Some of the best known haunts in the city
date back to the eighteenth century and are still thriving
(though some, it must be said, seem to thrive merely on
reputation). In any event, it is hard to get a bad cup of coffee
here and you can choose between the convivial atmosphere
of the local neighborhood cafe, the plush and sophisticated
surroundings of one of the historical cafes, or the outright
decadence of the likes of Caffè Platti or Norman.

There is almost a cult-like devotion to the cafe in Turin,
and for good reason — they offer coffee, football news, the
papers, and local gossip in the morning, drinks in the evening, and often serviceable food at lunchtime or at least
panini and *tramezzini*. Almost all cafes also feature evening snacks, called *stuzzichini* — if you pay for a drink you
are entitled to gorge on the decorously arranged piles of
cheese, *salumi*, olives, and bread. The aperitif hour begins
around 6:30 or 7 and seems to last until the *stuzzichini* run
out.

(Note that many wine shops become *enoteche* in the
late afternoon and evening, serving wine by the glass and
snacks. You can then buy a bottle from the shelves to take

home for dinner. Such establishments are listed in the Food and Wine section.)

AL BICERIN
Piazza della Consolata, 5 · ☎ 011.436.9325

Al Bicerin is listed in every piece of tourist literature about the city, and rightfully so. Despite the steep price for a seated *cafe normale*, the atmosphere is worth it if you can get a seat. The petite interior features eight small marble tables and dates from 1763. The cafe sits in the small Piazza della Consolata, and it is as pleasant to sit outside when the weather cooperates as inside the cozy room during the gray, cool months. The coffee is good, but visitors come for the heartstopping drink which gives the cafe its name: a concoction of coffee, whipped cream, and chocolate.

BAR MULASSANO
Piazza Castello, 9 · ☎ 011.547.990

Cheek-by-jowl with the much larger Baratti & Milano (see below), Mulassano—dating to 1909—is a miniature celebration of art nouveau. The marble counter is embedded with bronze panels, and there is intricate mahogany work on the walls and coffered leather ceilings. Unique and much loved by the Torinesi—a work of art that hasn't become a museum.

BARATTI & MILANO
Piazza Castello, 29 · ☎ *011.561.3060*

Located in the Galleria Subalpina since 1875 and expanded in 1909, the mahogany furniture and silk-covered walls of Baratti & Milano have welcomed many royals, and the place always looks as though it's expecting more to walk in. Today, decor intact, you can have a light lunch, coffee and cake, or an aperitif behind the glass windows looking out into the Galleria.

BAROLINO COCCHI
via Bonelli, 16/c · ☎ *011.436.7245*

Tarts, *tramezzini*, coffee, and drinks can be had at this tiny, circular bar along the shady, winding via Bonelli. Dating to the mid-eighteenth century, it's small enough that you may have to take your espresso outside. A perfect stop along the Quadrilatero walk.

CAFFÈ ELENA
Piazza Vittorio Veneto, 5/b · ☎ *011.812.3341*

This elegant cafe is tucked into a corner at the top of the piazza and has a real following among neighborhood residents, university students, and those beginning their long evenings at the clubs along the *murazzi*. The tables under the porticoes are an ideal spot for people watching in Piazza Vittorio, and a convenient spot for a quick lunch.

CAFFÈ NORMAN
via Pietro Micca, 22 · ☎ 011.540.854

Located at the end of via Pietro Micca, overlooking Piazza Solferino. Though much of its grand interior seems a bit stale today, the decadent decor and pyramid of *stuzzichini* at aperitif time are always pleasing to see. Open 24 hours a day (a real rarity in Turin) Thursday through Sunday.

CAFFÈ SAN CARLO
Piazza San Carlo, 156 · ☎ 011.532.586

Under the porticoes of the piazza of the same name, San Carlo was once the meeting place for the so-called "patriots," the liberal opponents of the conservatives (who met in Caffè Fiorio, in via Po) during the Risorgimento. Today, the gilt glory of the time remains intact and is still appreciated by locals and visitors alike.

CAFFÈ TORINO
Piazza San Carlo, 204 · ☎ 011.545.118

Like its neighbor across the piazza, Caffè Torino is luxurious and history hangs in the air: it was a favorite destination of statesman Luigi Einaudi and the novelist Cesare Pavese. As befits the location, prices for drinks and coffee can be steep.

LA DROGHERIA
Piazza Vittorio Veneto, 18 · ☎ 011.812.2414

An informal bar with several rooms, La Drogheria's charmingly mismatched furniture—dominated by an old wood and marble communal table in the center room—and simple decor are comfortable and unusual. They serve breakfast, light food at lunch, and cakes, coffee, and drinks throughout the day.

LE CANTINE BARBAROUX
via Barbaroux, 13 · ☎ 011.535.412

Swiftly becoming a neighborhood institution in the Quadrilatero, this may be my favorite place for *aperitivi*. Friendly, staunchly local, and neither slick nor modern, the dark rooms at Barbaroux (not to be confused with the nearby restaurant called Barbarus up the street) make a nice break at lunchtime, too. A small kitchen in the back sends out gorgeous plates of fresh and delicious cheeses, meats, and olives, perfect accompaniments to a glass of wine from their small but smart wine list.

SOCIÉTÉ LUTÈCE
Piazza Carlo Emanuele II, 21 · ☎ 011.887.644

In keeping with the slightly bohemian tone of Piazza Carlina, this popular French-inflected cafe attracts a youngish crowd in the evenings and a sizable audience for its limited, but inexpensive, lunchtime menu. It can sometimes seem as though it's the setting for a fashion shoot, but the informal bar atmosphere and outdoor tables are appealing.

TORTERIA OLSEN
via Sant'Agostino, 4/b · ☎ 011.436.1573
This tea house in the middle of the Quadrilatero makes a good rest stop during the day and serves a variety of Austrian-inspired cakes and teas, in addition to light lunch items (many of which are vegetarian). Cute and comfortable.

VINICOLA AL SORIJ
via Matteo Pescatore, 10 · ☎ 011.835.667
Vinicola al Sorij, between the Mole Antonelliana and Piazza Vittorio Veneto, is relatively new and already popular. Informal and tavern-like, the wine selection is broad and the service jovial; a comfortable spot for a glass of wine and a small meal.

RESTAURANTS

T HE REGIONAL COOKING OF NORTHWEST ITALY FINDS EXPRESSION IN THE RESTAU-rant kitchens of Turin—which, it could be said, doesn't really have a cuisine of its own. Restaurants owned by Cuneese, Astigiani, and Albanese families interpret Piedmontese classics, and nearly all keep standards high, ingredients local, and offer service at once warm and professional. Restaurants are required by law to close one day a week, typically Sunday or Monday. Lunch is generally served from 12:30 to 2:30, and dinner from 8:00 to 10:30 or 11:00 (a few restaurants stay open much later). Nearly all take most of August off.

There are hundreds of places to eat well in Turin; what follows is a very selective list. I have left out many of the high-end restaurants—even classic places like Ristorante del Cambio—which serve traditional Piedmontese food but do so in an atmosphere so formal as to sap some of the pleasure of the experience. Few Torinesi regularly eat at such places. I've also left out many of the newer, trendier establishments, which employ words like "inventive" and "modern" to draw attention away from exactly the qualities that seem to me to make Piedmontese food appealing—that it is hearty, unfussy, and flavorful; that it is inextricably linked to the land and the seasons; and that it is representative of traditions being lost everywhere to the demons of speed and convenience.

As in much of Italy, some of the best food in Turin is to be found in *trattorie* (small scale, family-run restaurants) or *osterie* (informal places that may not even have a written menu, which serve very simple and economical food), and not in the slick, dark wood and chrome paeans to modern design—of which there are increasing numbers throughout the city, established by a wave of young entrepreneurs and restauranteurs who, without a doubt, are providing more choice for locals, but who often eschew regional cuisine for the increasingly popular Spanish and Middle Eastern. There is even, at the time of writing, a Siberian restaurant in the Quadrilatero.

Some of the restaurants I include here might not appear exceptional from the outside, or even once you step through the door. What may seem like a lack of attention to decor can often mean more attention paid to the food and the service. Many places that seem plain from a visitor's perspective—and many *trattorie* may—are vital to their neighborhood, and you'll gain more from an evening's experience at, for example, Dai Saletta in San Salvario or L'osto del Borg Vej in the Quadrilatero, than one in stuffier confines.

Meals out in the evening are usually composed of three, if not more, courses: *primi*, *secondi* (with vegetable sides, or *contorni*), and *dolci* (desserts). You'd be forgiven for thinking this is too much food, especially if you've indulged in ample *stuzzichini* at the bar down the street just an hour or two before. As formal as Turin can be, ways are not so set that you will be looked at askance for ordering just a single plate of pasta or a main dish and a vegetable side. However, it would be a shame to skip a *dolce*. While cakes are not often eaten at home and are usually consigned to mid-afternoon coffee or tea at cafes, some traditional desserts appear on many menus; *bonet* (a chocolate and amaretti set pudding), the more familiar *panna cotta*, and fresh fruit are almost always offered, and there is always the option of the cheese cart, which presents an opportunity to taste a variety of artisanal Piedmontese cheeses.

But back to dinner! *Primi* are typically small plates of pasta, traditionally a *tajarin* or *agnolotti*; *risotto*; the soufflé-like *sformato* (often incorporating artichokes or asparagus, in season), or *vitello tonnato*—a dish of thinly sliced, cold veal smothered in a mayonnaise-tuna-caper sauce—a local specialty that I resisted for years, but have become dangerously addicted to. Main dishes can be wide-ranging. Proximity to Genoa guarantees much more fish on the menu than one might expect so close to the Alps (though locally-caught river trout is abundant), but the meaty mainstays are veal, rabbit, and the local specialties *bollito misto* and the wintery *brasato*. Few restaurants still serve the former in the traditional way, from a rolling cart brought to your tableside and carved in front of you; Tre Galline and La Capannina are good places to partake of this pleasing ritual. Don't be surprised to find snails and frog's legs on the menu. This is due less to French influence than the fact that both are by-products of the extensive rice fields of the Po river valley. Though less popular than they once were, both are still available in *trattorie* or *osterie* in the hills, or those restaurants that specialize in rustic fare. *Finanziera* and *fritto misto* are two other regional dishes worth looking for (and they sometimes need to be ordered in advance). The former is a combination of chicken organ meat and offal (including the cockscomb) in a meaty sauce; the latter (literally "fried mix") can include a combination of anything from slices of meat to whole fruit to cheese—all fried.

One way to try a number of local dishes without having to endure a multi-course meal every evening is to try *monopiatti*—single plate meals—at lunchtime. Many restaurants offer selections from their regular menu as a single dish or as part of a two-course meal at lunch. Almost always reasonably priced, a set lunch includes mineral water or a carafe of wine, coffee, and dessert.

Vegetarians are increasingly well-catered for and it is now common, even at the most traditional restaurants, to see at least one offering in each course without meat or fish. It is advised to ask, however, about the use of meat stocks and sauces in certain preparations if it is not explicitly clear that you are ordering a vegetarian dish.

Average price indications: € = less than €25 per person; €€ = €25–€40 per person; €€€ = €40–€75 per person for dinner, including wine. *Note that some restaurants at the higher end of this scale may be much more reasonable at lunchtime.*

PIEDMONTESE

AL GARAMOND
via Pomba, 14 · ☎ 011.812.2781
Closed Sat for lunch; Sun
€€€

The menu choices here may not be wholly typical, but the techniques are classic and even the more experimental dishes—especially fish—are exceptional. Probably the best choice among Turin's high-end restaurants if you want to splash out under brick vaulted ceilings and in period style.

AL REFETTORIO
via dei Mille, 23/D · ☎ 011.887.422
Closed Sun
€

A friendly and informal spot for a single-plate lunch or cake and coffee. You'll often see small groups of co-workers or single diners reading the paper in the peace and comfort of this neighborhood local. Simply decorated and without pretense, Al Refettorio offers good salads, usually one pasta dish, and particularly nice quiches and tarts. Order from the menu at the cash register or bar and take a seat in one of the dining rooms.

DAI SALETTA
via Belfiore, 37 · ☎ 011.668.7867
Closed Sun
€

This small and homey *trattoria* in San Salvario has exemplary local fare—homemade pasta, rabbit and brasato, and good desserts. Prices—including those on the Piedmontese wine list—are reasonable, especially at lunch.

GUGLIELMO PEPE
via Della Rocca, 19 · ☎ 011. 812.6843
Closed Sun
€

Facing the lovely Piazza Maria Vittorio—with tables out on the square in warm weather—this cafe serves good *monopiatti* lunches—a bargain at under €10 with water, wine, and coffee. The setting is refined, yet informal and the pasta and cold meat dishes are especially good. It also makes a convenient Borgo Nuova coffee stop in between gallery visits.

L'AGRIFOGLIO
via Accademia Albertina, 38/D · ☎ 011.837.064
Closed Sun and Mon
€€€

Impeccable cooking and a Piedmontese-only wine list make Adriano Pistorio's small L'Agrifoglio a favorite among Slow Food advocates. Slightly updated classic dishes showcase the finest and freshest ingredients available in season and despite rather high prices, there is a reasonable set menu (€28.50). Desserts are worth saving room for, but the cheese cart always holds the best in regional choices from artisanal producers. There are only ten tables, and it is necessary to book in advance.

LA BADESSA
Piazza Carlo Emanuele II, 17/h · ☎ 011.835.940
Closed Sun; Mon for lunch
€€

The food at the charming and modest La Badessa is inspired by age-old recipes developed in the monasteries of northern Italy. The dishes, while traditional and heavy on meat, have a light touch; try, for example, the *tagliatelle al ragù di coniglio e olive*. The downstairs dining room has a brick vaulted ceiling, while the ground floor is dominated by a painting of La Badessa (the "Mother Superior") herself and a stunning marble breakfront decorated with candles and flowers year round, which holds the tempting dessert and cheese selection. In the warm months, tables are set outside on Piazza Carlina, where at lunchtime tables are shoved together to accommodate families elbow-to-elbow with business meetings.

LA CAPANNINA
via Donati, 1 · ☎ *011.545.405*
Closed Sun

€€

The rustic dining room here is an amateur collector's delight: hanging from the walls are saxophones, french horns, Alpine hats, alarm clocks, stag heads, copper pots and pans…The food, while it might be rustic, is not only a superb offering of cuisine from the Langhe, but is served traditionally—*bollito misto* from the cart, *agnolotti del plin* in *sugo arrosto* brought to your table in its saucepan. The wine list isn't long, but has many fairly priced, and some unusual, Piedmontese bottles. Via Donati is on a thick residential block close to Corso Vittorio Emanuele II, a bit off the beaten path but easy to find.

LA TAVERNA DI FRA FIUSCH
Via Beria, 32 (Revigliasco) · ☎ *011.860.8224*
Closed Mon; serves dinner only Tues—Fri

€€€

Fra Fiusch is nearly impossible to get to without a car and difficult to find even if you have one; but the twenty-five-minute journey is part of the pleasure of this hilltop restaurant just above Moncalieri. Beautiful views from the upstairs rooms, a fireplace downstairs, welcoming service, and a reasonably priced wine list make Fra Fiusch a joy all around. They prepare *finaziera* and *fritto misto* on the weekend, both of which are superb—but need to be reserved in advance. And definitely book ahead for a table, in any case.

LE TRE GALLI
via Sant'Agostino, 25 · ☎ 011.521.6027
Closed Sun
€€

An early entrant in the gentrification of the neighborhood, Tre Galli's airy dining room and attractive outdoor tables topped with butcher-paper along this short, pedestrianized street have won many fans (perhaps also because it's open until 2am). Simply and beautifully decorated, it offers a small, well-prepared menu of Piedmontese standards.

LE VITEL ETONNÉ
via San Francesco da Paola, 4 · ☎ 011.812.4621
Closed Sun; Wed for lunch
€

A popular spot for *aperitivi* and light dinners. The local dish in the French name ("veal in tuna sauce") is always available, and quite good. A large wine list offers good options by the glass and there's a nice selection of cheese for either after dinner or with *aperitivi*.

L'OSTO DEL BORG VEJ
Via Tassi Torquai, 7 · ☎ 011.436.4843
Closed Sun
€€

This family-run *osteria* seats less than fifty in charming, curtained ground- and second-floor dining rooms—tastefully and simply furnished, intimate, and just a little bit formal. Antique photographs of Turin grace the walls. Reasonably priced set menus come in three options and the small wine list is mainly Piedmontese with a few selections from other regions. Try their *agnolotti del plin* and *vitello tonnato*. It is necessary to book for dinner (and to ring the bell to get in!).

MONFERRATO
via Monferrato, 6 · ☎ 011.819.0661
Closed Sun; dinner only Sat
€€

Near Gran Madre in the Borgo Po, Monferrato is in my opinion by far one of the best restaurants in the city. Impeccable, old-fashioned service from a friendly staff and a comfortable, pleasing dining room inspire instant ease. Excellent pasta dishes including *tajarin* with mushrooms, *agnolotti del plin al sugo di arrosto*, classic desserts, and a wine list not limited to Piedmontese selections round out an impeccable experience.

PERBACCO

via Mazzini, 31 · ☎ *011.882.110*
Closed Sun; serves dinner only
€€

Roberto Perego's refined yet easygoing restaurant in the Borgo Nuovo is warm and inviting, a comfortable place to while away an indulgent dinner. It also stays open late, and there always seems to be a party coming in just when you expect the lights to be turned off. Perego will probably take your order himself, and sit beside you to describe the dishes on offer and recommend wines. The service is efficient and professional without being cold. Wonderful Piedmontese dishes are served here (and the fish is superb and sometimes prepared in unusual ways).

PORTA DI SAVONA

Piazza Vittorio Veneto, 2 · ☎ *011.817.3500*
Closed Mon; Tues for lunch
€€

This popular *trattoria* has tables out on the piazza in clement weather, and the buoyant atmosphere and handsome decor—old photos of Turin, wood paneling—make up for only slightly-better-than-average local fare. *Monopiatti* are a good deal at lunchtime, when the service is slightly less hectic than during the dinner rush.

SAVOIA

via Corte d'Appello, 13 · ☎ *011.436.2228*
Closed Sat lunch; Sun

€€€

Elegant and a little coy (there's no sign; look for the menu
in the window), Savoia is just around the corner from the
Palazzo Barolo. There are two set menus, both rather pricey,
but the rooms are classic, the food carefully prepared, and
the service discreet without being haughty. If you book
ahead you can request a vegetarian set dinner.

SOTTO LA MOLE

via Montebello, 9 · ☎ *011.817.9398*
Closed Sun for lunch; Tues and Wed

€€€

The set meals are priced a little high, but the *agnolotti* is
superb. The menu is mainly Piedmontese but mixes in
some Tuscan fare. The location—almost literally "under
the Mole"—is good, too, especially if you're ending your
day at the cinema museum, with a movie at the Massimo,
or over *aperitivi* at nearby Vinicola al Sorij.

SPADA REALE

via Principe Amedeo, 53 · ☎ *011.817.1363*
Closed Sun

€€

This warm restaurant, which has a Tuscan touch to the
menu, has been a favorite for years, especially with RAI

employees who work nearby. It is always crowded—you may wind up bumping chairs with diners at the next table—but it's the kind of place where nobody minds, and the service is attentive on even the busiest nights.

TORRICELLI
via Torricelli, 51 · ☎ *011.599.814*
Closed Sun; Mon for lunch
€€

Torricelli is almost too good to be a neighborhood place, which is what it feels like, in clientele and decor. On weekends, it gets crowded and it is clear that its reputation is not confined to the Crocetta locals and that the simple room doesn't detract from its good fish selection and homemade pasta dishes.

TRATTORIA CON CALMA
Strada Comunale del Cartman, 59 · ☎ *011.898.0229*
Closed Mon; serves dinner only Tues−Sat
€€€

On the way towards Superga and up into the hills, Con Calma rests in a lovely countrified spot. The dining room has a log fire and there is outdoor seating year round. Superb but expensive, it is a good choice for provincial fare without heading to the countryside.

TRATTORIA VALENZA
via Borgo Dora, 39 · ☎ 011.521.3914
Closed Sun
€

Conveniently located for lunch on market Saturdays, the wood-panelled Valenza appears to be decorated with bits and pieces from the market itself. Informal, with a regular clientele, Valenza is good for no-frills, *trattoria* fare. Pastas, homemade *cottechino*, and *bagna cauda* are excellent. It gets busy during the Balon, so book ahead.

TRE GALLINE
via Bellezia, 37 · ☎ 011.436.6553
Closed Sun; Mon for lunch
€€

Le Tre Galline, virtually unchanged in a neighborhood undergoing rapid development and just a short distance from Porta Palazzo, is one of the most traditional restaurants in the city. The classics are done well here, including *bollito misto* (which will be delivered to your table properly on a rolling cart), pastas, and roast meat dishes. The quiet, elegant atmosphere and discreet service makes Tre Galline a nice spot for an intimate lunch after the cheerful chaos of the Porta Palazzo market up the street. There is also a fine wine list and well-priced set lunches.

PIZZA

AMICI MIEI
Corso Vittorio Emanuele II, 94 · ☎ 011.506.9961
Closed for lunch Sat and Sun
€€

A popular pizzeria located under the porticoes—great for a family outing or when the formality of Turin's restaurants begins to wear. It is near the GAM, where dining options are otherwise thin.

IL ROSPETTO
Piazza Madama Cristina, 5 · ☎ 011.669.8221
Closed Mon
€

One of the best pizzerias in the city. Open only in the evenings and a bit small, it is extremely popular, especially on the weekends. Unusually, the pizzas are made in an electric pizza oven, drawing criticism from some purists, though you wouldn't be able to tell from the crowds. Specialities include (very) thin crust pizza, foccaccia di Recco, and desserts made in-house.

LA GARGANICA
via Carlo Alberto, 18 · ☎ 011.538.889
Closed Sat and Sun for lunch; Mon
€

Well-priced family run neighborhood pizzeria in the

center of town. The *farinata* (a chickpea-flour pancake, not unlike French *socca*) is particularly good here, as are the margherita pizzas. It's small and closed in the afternoons. An inexpensive option in the evenings if you're staying nearby.

PIZZERIA ALLA BAITA DEI SETTE NANI
via Andrea Doria, 5 · ☎ 011.535.812
Closed Mon
€

Expect a wait, especially on weekend evenings, when the ten woodhewn tables and benches at this popular spot—the "chalet of the seven dwarves"—fill with local families. The small pizzas are baked in the enormous oven at the back of the room, but it's the *farinata* that you come for—some of the best around. There are also a few hearty main courses, such as *salsiccia* served with white beans and *lasagna al forno*, if you're not in the mood for pizza.

SAINT PAUL
Corso Vittorio Emanuele II, 45 · ☎ 011.669.3935
Closed Mon
€€

Not far from Porta Nuova, this relatively new, slick pizzeria serves excellent thin crust pies that are baked on a layer of salt. Popular with the visiting business crowd in the evenings, so it's best to book for dinner.

SPACCANAPOLI
via Mazzini, 19 · ☎ *011.812.6694*
Closed Tues
€€

A surprisingly popular Neopolitan pizzeria (perhaps because of rumors that footballers congregate here), but convenient for the museums and fun with kids. The pizza is good, there's beer on tap, and the service is cheerful, if hectic.

ANTICHI FOCACCERIA GENOVESE
via Perrone, 2
& via San Domenico, 13
€

There are an abundance of Ligurian *focaccerie* around town (look for the green-and-yellow signs) which are useful in fending off hunger throughout the day or as a small substitute for lunch. The two outlets above serve a superior product, and the one on San Domenico is open on Sundays.

SAINT TOMMASO BREAK
via San Tomasso, 2/d
€

Near the Piazza Castello end of via Garibaldi (from which you'll be able to see Saint Tomasso's sign and the line forming at the window counter); pizza slices hot from the oven and wrapped for walking.

FOREIGN CUISINE

EL MIR
Piazza Corpus Domini, 17 · ☎ 011.562.4496
Closed Sun
€

The Lebanese menu here is considered some of the best ethnic food in the city.

Near the Piazza Palazzo di Città and Porta Palatina, it's a good spot for trips through the Quadrilatero, to the Museo di Antichità, or if you simply want a change of pace from Italian food. Ingredients are fresh and the hummous, kebabs, and the homemade bread are especially good.

HAFA
via Sant'Agostino, 23/c · ☎ 011.436.7091
Closed Mon
€€

Open late—usually until 1 or 2am—Hafa serves tasty plates of Moroccan and Algerian cuisine. A great place for a cocktail or coffee, it is decorated with traditional low tables, cushions, and lanterns (there are ordinary tables in the main room and outside, as well). A sunken room in the back is quiet and intimate and the service friendly, outgoing, and multi-lingual. Traditional mixed platters, tagines, and couscous are served at lunch and dinner.

KIKI

via della Rocca, 39/g · ☎ *011.835.084*
Closed Mon
€€€

True sushi in the Borgo Nuovo. Kiki serves reasonably priced mixed sushi platters, à la carte sushi and sashimi, and traditional Japanese dishes in a light, refined, modern atmosphere alongside an extensive wine list.

KIRKUK CAFE

via Carlo Alberto, 16bis/A · ☎ *011.530.657*
Closed Sun
€

Kirkuk, run by couple Fuad and Giulia, serves Kurdish, Turkish, and other Middle Eastern food in an informal dining room. Centrally located close to Piazza San Carlo and Piazza Carignano, it has friendly service, good Turkish coffee, and affordable prices—two can have lunch for under €15.

MARHABA

via San Domenico, 12 · ☎ *011.521.4452*
Closed for lunch Fri
€

Low prices keep this welcoming, Egyptian-run *trattoria* constantly busy. The Egyptian, Lebanese, and Syrian food is fresh and service attentive.

GELATO

IT IS HARDLY AN EXAGGERATION TO SAY
THAT A VISITOR TO TURIN COULD EAT
gelato twice a day for a week and not repeat a visit
to the same *gelateria*—or be sated. Though to some
(me among them) this is a dreamy proposition, it
would be a shame to subject yourself to some of
the factory produced, artifcially flavored goop that
passes as gelato at some establishments—recognizable by their neon colors and plastic tubs.

Gelato was first made for the court of Francesco
de' Medici in the sixteenth century, by Bernardo
Buontalenti. Different from American ice cream
in numerous ways, gelato is a combination of whole
milk, eggs, sugar, and flavoring (fruit gelati are
simply fresh fruit and sugar). Less firmly frozen
and more intensely flavored than ice cream, gelato
has no air whipped into it in the making process and
is much smoother than ice cream. It is increasingly
common to see gelato made with soy milk, so those
who typically go without dairy need not despair.

There are endless flavors to suit everyone, but

no one should miss out on the *nocciola* or *cioccolato* while in Piedmont, or the gelati made from Sicilian lemons, or local pears, or the heavenly *fior di latte*— an "unflavored flavor" that allows the best qualities of fresh Piedmontese milk and cream to stand out and is sometimes served alongside fresh summer berries in restaurants. It's unusual to order just one flavor and unseemly to order more than three, so combine flavors such as *cioccolato* and *crema*; *fior di latte* and a fruit; *nocciola* and *cioccolato*; or *crema* and strawberry. What follows is a select list of the finer artisanal gelato establishments marked by the evident pride in their production and ingredients, as well as by the charm of their locales.

FIORIO
via Po, 8 · ☎ 011.817.3225
A historic cafe that was the favored haunt of Cavour, the Piedmontese statesman and architect of nationhood, and other politicians in the nineteenth century, but today it is gelato rather than political talk that attracts most. Fiorio's gelato has good flavor and a lot of fans, but is perhaps a bit too smooth. On warm days, the queue at the window can get quite competitive!

GROM
Piazza Paleocapa, 1/d · ☎ 011.511.9067

GROM's motto is *crema come una volta*, or "gelato as it used to be," and if the crowds here are any indication, gelato used to be better. Their *fior di latte* is like very cold whipped cream; their three kinds of chocolate are all made with organic Venezuelan cocoa. GROM may be the most expensive gelato in the city, but it's worth every penny. One month, their special flavor combination was pear and chocolate, and my husband insists that their crema is the best in town. Near many of the Centro hotels, and close to Porta Nuova.

LATTERIA TESTA, 56
via Re Umberto · ☎ 011.599.775

In addition to fulfilling its role as a neighborhood *latteria*—selling butter, cream, and *crema montata* (whipped cream), Testa also makes gelato that draws fans from all over the city. In a recent *La Stampa* "Gelato Dream" column, Testa received a glowing recommendation. An "o" shaped magnet beside a menu of flavors indicates what's available that day. A good stop in the Crocetta district or after a visit to the GAM.

MIRETTI
Corso Matteotti, 5 · ☎ 011.533.687

It's not unusual to find a line forming at Cafe Miretti's gelato window soon after lunch or when the nearby offices disgorge their workers at the end of the day, when many Torinesi have a gelato to bridge the time before the evening meal. Miretti has a high reputation and the *fior di latte* is incomparable. The gelato window is attached to a lovely cafe, popular in and of itself.

PEPINO
Piazza Carignano, 8 · ☎ 011.542.009

Aside from being strategically located in my favorite spot in the city, Pepino has the added bonus of offering some of the finest gelato in Turin. The location of their charming, almost hidden gelato window is no secret to young and old alike—it's not unusual to see busloads of school children lining up after a visit to the Museo di Risorgimento across the street. Pepino's flavors retain just enough texture to remind you of your chosen flavor. Fruit gelati are superb; coconut, raspberry, and pear taste only of real fruit. Get your *cono* or *coppa*, printed with Pepino's *nouveau* blue logo, sit in Piazza Carignano, gaze at the Palazzo, and watch the city pass by.

SHOPS

TURIN IS A CITY OF SHOPKEEPERS. BUT MOST SHOPKEEPERS THERE AREN'T MERELY shop owners—they are the designers, artisans, tailors, cheesemakers, and bookbinders behind the shops. Many businesses have been in families for years and the pride people take in their trades is obvious. Some shopkeepers almost expect that you know what you want, that you'll want them to help you find it, and that you intend to buy it (bookstores are something of an exception). I've sometimes felt a little intimidated simply browsing, but a friendly "*solo dare un occhiata*"—just looking—usually does the trick. The city is full of remarkable bookshops (Mark Twain observed on a visit: "Turin must surely read a good deal, for it has more bookstores to the square rod than any other town I know of... ."), independent designers, and artisans, who are often willing to talk to you about their work and always seem pleased you've stopped in. Here, as throughout Italy, it's customary to greet the shopkeeper and thank them when you leave, whether you've interacted with them or not; not doing so can appear rude.

Throughout Turin there is a steady parade of *camicierie*—shirtmakers. Each neighborhood, it seems, has at least two or three shops where made-to-measure shirts can be ordered up in a week or two's time. Still mainly a men's service, more and more shirtmakers are catering to women, though the styles may seem a touch conservative. In any event, having a few shirts custom made on your trip is a nice way to bring a piece of local craftsmanship back with you, and it will not likely break the bank.

Nearly all shops in Turin are open between 10:00 am and 12:30 pm, close for lunch, and then reopen from 2:30 or 3:00 pm until 7:30 or 8:00 pm. Sunday openings are almost unheard of (except around Christmas, when many shops put on holiday hours for a few weeks). Also note that many shops, if they open at all on Monday, do so only after lunch.

In the Centro and in shopping districts such as via Garibaldi, the encroachment of chain stores is readily apparent. Though increasingly made up of the banal international shops familiar everywhere else, Turin still boasts a handful of small, homegrown chains—mainly clothing stores, such as GB Sportelli and Katherine Klee—where, in true Italian fashion, quality and style are paramount. But the local is still vital to the city and its unique character. Below are some of my favorite, mainly independently-owned, shops.

BOOKS

AGORÀ
via San Croce, 0/e · ☎ *011.835.973*
Steps from Piazza Carlina is this specialist art and design bookstore owned by Bruno Boveri (who is, by the way, closely involved with the Slow Food movement) and Rosalba Spit-

aleri. The front of the store features mostly photography titles, while the back room, with its unusual metal shelving, holds new and used titles in art, interior design, and gardening, in addition to books for students in advertising and design. The attached gallery exhibits photography curated by the proprietors.

COMUNARDI
via Bogino, 2 · ☎ *011.817.0036*

Close to via Po and in the shadow of the Biblioteca Nazionale, Comunardi's selection of new political non-fiction and cinema books hides behind a plain facade. The store has a decidedly leftist slant, and an especially good selection of film and literary magazines, along with Italian graphic novels.

FELTRINELLI
via Piazza Castello, 19 · ☎ *011.541.627*
& via Roma, 80 · ☎ *011.534.4914*

The mega-sized via Roma branch of this publisher's retail operation (head toward the giant neon *La Stampa* sign) is pleasantly overwhelming, despite being one of the few corporate-owned bookstores in a city full of independents. There are exhaustive sections on travel (especially at the Piazza Castello shop), Italian history, current affairs, and classic Italian literature, in addition to all the new titles on the tables up front, arranged by publisher—as is typical in many Italian bookstores. There is also a wide array of

Italian and international magazines and newspapers.

FOGOLÀ
Piazza Carlo Felice, 15 · ☎ 011.562.9171

Fogolà's carpeted floors, wood tables, and vaulted ceilings downstairs recall Torino's literary heyday. Founded in 1911, it is one of the older bookstores in the city, and its narrow corridors and toppling towers of books add to the old-fashioned atmosphere. The store offers a wall full of old and new books on local history, as well as a strong art section and an upstairs art gallery featuring occasional exhibitions of regionally recognized artists.

FRANCO MARIA RICCI
via Carlo Alberto, 12/e · ☎ 011.562.9171

The retail storefront of the publisher of *FMR* magazine offers the magazine and fine art books published under that name in addition to the limited-edition, hand-printed "Pulcino Elefante" series of artist's books.

GILIBERT ARTE E LETTERE
via Bonelli, 4/c · ☎ 011.436.3891
& Galleria Subalpina, 17 · ☎ 011.561.9225

The via Bonelli branch of Gilibert has just three simple white rooms, unlike the more refined gallery setting of the Galleria Subalpina shop. It specializes in twentieth-century illustrated books on art and film, and has racks of antique advertising posters and prints for sale.

IL CARTIGLIO
via Po, 32 · ☎ *011.817.9005*

Founded in 1985 in a nineteenth-century shopfront, Roberto Cena stocks an extraordinary collection of Piedmontese and Torinese engravings, prints, maps, and books. Come here to find centuries-old, out-of-print guidebooks to the city and engravings of Turin dating to the 1700s.

IL MONDO DELLE MERAVIGLIE
via Accademia Albertina, 36 · ☎ *011.883.441*

This well-stocked children's bookstore—the books seem almost to reach the ceiling—has one of the friendliest staffs in town and is a pleasure for children, parents, and gift-seekers alike. You can find anything from Italo Calvino's classic three-volume collection of Italian folktales to a vast array of contemporary European illustrated children's books to Richard Scarry's books for young readers in Italian.

IL MONDO IN TASCA
via Montebello, 22/C · ☎ *011.888.140*

A lovely and simple store—its name means "the world in your pocket"—practically under the Mole Antonelliana and close to the university. Its one room features well-chosen books for travellers in English and Italian, including contemporary and classic travel writing, travel guidebooks to destinations all over the world, coffee-table books, maps, and more.

JULES ET JIM
via Bogino, 19 · ☎ 011.836.402

In a street already rich with art galleries and cafes, Jules et Jim is a charming bolt-hole stacked floor to ceiling with new and used books on cinema.

LIBRERIA ANTIQUARIA PREGLIASCO
via Accademia Albertina, 3/bis · ☎ 011.817.7114

Near the via Po and in business since 1913, Pregliasco's selection can be rarefied and pricey, but it is consistently stocked with antique maps, architectural prints, works on paper by Piedmontese artists, and early books about Turin and the region.

LIBRERIA FONTANA
via Monte di Pietà, 19 · ☎ 011.542.924

Fontana, artfully designed by Stefano Pajot and Simone Carena, is a modern and pleasing shop well-stocked with new releases and classics. It has particulary good travel and local Turin sections and plenty of children's books. They also regularly host events with local authors.

LIBRARIE VOYELLES DE LA FRANCOPHONIE
via San Massimo, 9 · ☎ 011.892.2978

The existence of two French language bookshops in Turin is a testament to the enduring French influence on the city. This is the newer of them, and the small shop sports fresh flower arrangements and exposed brick walls in addition to its stock of new books from France.

LUXEMBOURG
via Accademia delle Scienze, 3/i · ☎ *011.561.3896*

One of the best bookstores in the city, in one of the finest locations in the city—at the edge of Piazza Carignano. Luxembourg carries a good stock of English-language novels and classics upstairs; a broad selection of new books in Italian with rich travel, food, and gay sections; and a broad selection of international magazines and newspapers, including the *New York Times.*

MOOD LIBRI E CAFFÈ
via Cesare Battisti, 3/e · ☎ *011.566.0809*

A combined bookstore and cafe, Mood is one of the newest and most fashionable establishments in Turin. The lively *aperitivi* scene here spills out into the piazza in the evenings. The space was designed by architect Giorgio Rosental, and owner Luca Ragagnin is often in the shop. Despite its trendiness, it's an ideal place to stop for a late afternoon or early evening drink—and a browse.

OOLP
via Principe Amedeo, 29 · ☎ *011.812.2782*

Near the art academy and the university, OOLP is an essential store for art book collectors. Giovanna Sartori's pleasantly packed shop, which grew out of the independent art and poetry publisher Out of London Press in the 1970s, carries new and used art books, with painting, sculpture, and gardens especially well represented.

TORRE DI ABELE
via Pietro Micca, 22 · ☎ 011.562.1407

At the end of Pietro Micca, near Piazza Solferino, is this informal and incredibly well-stocked shop that nonetheless retains an independent, old-fashioned feel. The ground floor has an especially good selection of new books on contemporary affairs and politics, as well as a wide selection of Italian literary and political journals. A great children's and travel section is downstairs, where events and readings are also held.

SHIRTMAKERS

BI & BI DI GIUSEPE BAIARDI
via Monferrato, 23 · ☎ 011.819.3619
& corso De Gasperi, 25 · ☎ 011.561.9229

Giuseppe Baiardi has a few shops throughout the city, but these two are calm places to buy his fine custom or off-the-peg shirts for men.

CAMICERIA DM
via Della Rocca, 32 · ☎ 011.885.795

Bolts of shirtcloth line the wood-panelled walls of this trusted Borgo Nuovo shop. They also do a brisk business in fine ties—custom and off-the-peg.

LORAN CAMICERIE
via Corte d'Appello, 13/p · ☎ 011.436.6923

A shop with nothing but a counter, bolts of fabric, and a workshop in the back. Good selection of materials for custom shirts, ties, boxer shorts, and handkerchiefs.

SEBASTIAN
via Cavour, 15 · ☎ 011.562.9696

Not as old a shop as some of the other classic shirtmakers in the city, Sebastian is a comfortable store selling fine off-the-peg and tailor-made shirts for men and women, with a vast array of collar, cuff, and color options.

SIMONA BRUNO
via San Francesco d'Assisi, 28/a · No phone

Custom shirts for men and women are available at Ms. Bruno's small shop on a wonderful street of bijoux stores. Some of her fabrics and designs are perhaps more adventurous than her counterparts' elsewhere in the city.

CLOTHING AND JEWELERY

AUTOPSIE VESTAMENTAIRE
via Bonelli, 6/B · ☎ 011.436.0641

Alice Capelli opened her laboratory of a shop in 2000 on via Bonelli, where her neighbors include the equally experimental Walter Dang and Galeria Pia's. Her unique sculptural pieces often incorporate antique fabrics and are all hand-made.

DAGARÀ
via Lagrange, 1/a · ☎ 011.544.701

The relatively new Dagarà carries handmade bags in classic
and unusual designs using only the finest Italian leather.
Prices are extremely reasonable given the workmanship,
variety, and range of colors and materials.

DOZO
via Po, 15 · ☎ 011.812.8476

Well-designed and stylish underwear and sleepwear for
men and women in basic colors, appealing patterns, and
mercerized cotton. A simple and tasteful store filled with
high-quality garments.

GALERIA PIA'S
via Bonelli, 11/a · ☎ 011.436.1579

In an area beginning to burst with young design talent and
attractive shops, Galeria Pia's carries in-house and locally-
designed garments and accessories for women chosen by
partners Silvia and Alessia. Daring and unique, but still
wearable, the selection is displayed in an atelier-like atmosphere.

IL SOGNO
via Sant'Agostino, 23/h · ☎ 011.436.5669

Couture wedding dresses in a corner of the Quadilatero

becoming known for its unusual shops. The sophisticated and sculptural dresses are artworks in and of themselves. They also design bespoke head-pieces and other wedding accesories.

JACK EMERSON
via Cesare Battisti, 1 · ☎ 011.562.1960

A pleasing bastion of elegance and tailoring, and a temple to Turin's age-old Anglophilia. Suits made from English wool can be made to order and there is an off-the-peg selection of English-style jackets (and capes) for men and women.

JANA
via Maria Vittoria, 45/a · ☎ 011.885.495

Jana's spartan shop features offerings from designers like Comme de Garçons, If 6 Was 9, Martin Margiela, and Carpe Diem. Owner Alda's consistently good taste is apparent from the moment you enter, and she carries only a limited number of each design.

KRISTINA T
via Maria Vittoria, 18 · ☎ 011.837.170

Turin native Cristina Tardito's long, light-filled shop has parquet floors, white walls, minimal fixtures, and often one of the most elegant window displays in the city. The crisp, but not unwelcoming setting is a perfect backdrop for her delicate women's clothing and lingerie. Beautiful sweaters and gossamer-thin dresses have a vintage feel, but are very stylish with a flattering cut.

LA BOA
via Carlo Alberto, 24 · ☎ 011.562.2496

This sophisticated, quiet boutique offers attentive and friendly service. The selection of smaller Italian designers is well-chosen and tasteful, and often unusual: well-cut dresses, skirts, and sweaters, but also great hats and bags. Stylish elegance without formality.

LA TERRA DELLE DONNE
via San Domenico, 18 · No phone

In the heart of the Quadrilatero this sweet vintage shop offers well-chosen clothing, accessories, and modestly-priced antique knick-knacks. Especially good for mid-century bags and unusual hats.

SAN LORENZO
via Des Ambrois, 7 · ☎ 011.883.531

A well-edited, limited selection of pieces from international and Italian designers are showcased in this smart, expensive shop. Service, as often in Turin, can be reserved, but it is always helpful.

SCOTTI GIOELLI
Piazza Vittorio Veneto, 10/f · No phone

A relatively new addition to Turin's collection of minimalist jewelery stores. On a recent visit, they were featuring an unusual selection of jade pieces draped over small Chinese statuary. Unique, sculptural pieces.

SEDICILUISAEFRANCHINO
via IV Marzo, 14/a · ☎ *011.433.8638*

An unusual marriage of haircut salon, housewares shop, and handmade clothes boutique. The customized dresses and shirts made in the workshop behind the salon area are one-of-a-kind without being too weird, and the atmosphere is playful without being silly.

SERIENUMERICA
via Bonelli, 4/c · ☎ *011.436.9644*

Inspired by Japanese clothing design, Maria De Ambrogio and Rosella Lavatelli's small shop features minimally designed, simply displayed clothing for women (and a small line of men's shirts). Each model is produced in a limited quantity and hung in the gallery-like space according to color. An adventurous range of garments—straight lines, quality tailoring, and a monochrome palette, with a few unusual patterns thrown into the mix—that you won't see everyone wearing... but that aren't unwearable.

STICKY FINGERS
via delle Orfane, 22/d · ☎ *011.521.7320*

An American-style vintage store with clothing from the 1950s to the 1970s for men and women. The varied stock changes often and is especially good for dresses, men's jackets, and accessories.

TOM-THUMB
Piazza Vittorio Veneto, 20/a · ☎ 011.883.826
& via Carlo Alberto, 31/a · ☎ 011.518.6654

Marzia Scabello's men's clothing stores carry slim-cut, well-made Italian suits, shirts, and separates in updated classic styles. It's hard to go wrong here if you're looking for a less expensive option to deisgner or bespoke, without skimping on quality. Marzia and her staff are always warm and good-humored, and they handle alterations with finesse and speed. (Plus there's an outlet shop on via Bonafus!)

INSTITUTO RICERCE APPLICAZIONI COSMESI
via San Massimo, 12 · ☎ 011.888.688

Paola Cobianchi's shop sells hair and skincare products that follow early nineteenth-century recipes created for the Savoys. Antique display cases, marble countertops, and simple packaging recall Turin's classic pharmacies, but the pale green walls and fresh flowers soften the touch. Soy, macadamia, and ginseng face creams and camomile and balsam shampoos are superb and subtly fragranced.

KIDS

CENTRO GIOCO EDUCATIVO
Via Cernaia, 25 · ☎ 011.541.776

As the name implies, educational toys are the name of the game here, but they also sell a variety of old-fashioned wooden games and toys.

IL GUFO
via De Gasperi, 35/f · ☎ 011.580.6119

A lovely Crocetta shop selling bright, tasteful clothing for infants to ten-year-olds. Popular and welcoming, it manages not to overdo the cute or treacly.

ISACCO
Corso Vittorio Emanuele II, 36 · ☎ 011.817.8485

This model train retailer has been a fixture on Vittorio Emanuele II for decades. Not just for children or serious adult collectors, the displays and selection of rare and unusual models are a treat for anyone.

WAWA AND DADA
via Bonelli, 8 · ☎ 011.438.0094

The owners of Atelier Walter Dang make and sell children's clothes at this small shop down the street from their women's couture studio. The colorful clothes are delightful without being too radical for adults or too weird for kids.

DESIGN & HOME FURNISHINGS

CARTABELLA
via Cavour, 13/nel cortile · ☎ 011.543.027

This courtyard studio workshop owned by Dario Coppo binds its own photo albums, blank books, and address books, and also sells a small selection of premade items. The creative atmosphere and truly handmade appeal make this a pleasant and unusual place for a unique gift. Dario takes special orders and makes bespoke pieces from the vast array of papers, leathers, and techniques at his disposal. Dario's custom, exquisite, hand-bound photo albums start at around €50 depending on page count and paper.

CINQUE
via Carlo Alberto, 5 · ☎ 011.836.574

The unusual, custom display cases at Cinque are the creation of Cristina De Ambrosis and Ferdi Giardini and hold a selection of imported housewares and objects: African baskets made from telephone wire, teas and soaps from around the world, Japanese teapots, and local honeys.

DE CARLO
via Cesare Battisti, 5 · ☎ 011.561.3378

A Turin insitution, De Carlo cutlery is beautifully designed and well-crafted, and a set of their wood-handled cheese knives makes a good gift or souvenir. They also carry a wide assortment of Italian and international designer kitchen and homeware, including a huge selection of espresso machines and pots.

HAFA
via Santa Chiara, 18/a · ☎ 011.436.2899

Hafa carries an interesting selection of home furnishings from the Middle East next door to its popular restaurant and cafe of the same name. Lights, pillows, and small housewares dominate the Maghreb-themed corner shop.

MERCATO DEI FIORI
Via Perugia, 29 · No phone

Across the Dora, jovial flower dealers throw open their stalls from 7–10 am and display a wild assortment of flora, making a trip here an invigorating morning project. The best way to arrive is by crossing the river at Ponte Regio Parco on foot or by the number 27 bus, which will leave you within a block of the market.

SLOBS 2
Piazza Carlo Emanuele II, 19/a · ☎ 011.836.003

Describing itself as a "home gallery," Slobs 2 carries a well-curated collection of modern European furniture in a nicely designed space in Piazza Carlina. A mix of Italian design classics, avant-garde work by new designers, and a small selection of antiques are artfully displayed side-by-side.

UNOMI
via Bonelli, 1/a · ☎ 011.335.830.0084

Hand-thrown and glazed dishes, bowls, and ceramic ware by Cristina Boselli are casually displayed in her workshop-cum-store. Her Japanese-inspired work is tasteful, a world apart from the dull, mass-produced imports that dominate housewares today.

ANTIQUES

IL BALON MARKET

For the weekend visitor to Turin with even a casual interest in antiques, a visit to Il Balon is a must. The winding streets behind Porta Palazzo fill with vendors and buyers every Saturday throughout the year (and swell further still with the Gran Balon, on the second Sunday of each month). The streets and alleyways are also home to a variety of furniture restorers, dealers, workshops, and small cafes and *osterie* that overflow on the weekends. Bargains may be hard to come by these days at Il Balon, but the stalls make good browsing for unusual pieces of jewelery, bric-a-brac, and prints, postcards, and books about Turin.

ANTIQUARIATO SCIENTIFICO E CURIOSITÀ D'EPOCA
via Bellezia, 15/b · ☎ 011.339.534.2312

Appropriate to the mysterious, winding streets of its Quadrilatero neighborhood, this cabinet of curiosities offers taxidermy animals, antique gyroscopes, and nineteenth-century medical models. Too small to get lost in, but endlessly enthralling.

BOTTEGA IL MARZO
via Torquato Tasso, 11 · ☎ 011.339.333.7653

The interior of this miniature flower and antiques store resembles a ramshackle garden shed, where rustic Italian and French antiques spill over the wide plank floor. They also create imaginative flower arrangements for special occassions.

FITZCARRALDO
via San Francesco d'Assisi, 24/g · ☎ 011.538.982

The petite Fitzcarraldo sells a tasteful selection of old and new: colorful bijoux jewelery from Milan-based Granievaghi, biscuit tins from the 1930s and 1940s, pottery and porcelain, antique toys, and other small collectibles.

GALLERIA CRISTIANI
via Maria Vittoria, 41 · ☎ 011.817.8391

The sister store to 13 Porta Palatina (below), Cristiani offers noteworthy furniture and objects ranging from Aalto table and chair sets to Italian lamps and the occasional larger architectural salvage piece.

GALLERIA LUIGI CARETTO
via Maria Vittoria, 10 · ☎ 011.537.274

On a street festooned with Piedmontese flags and lined with antiques shops, Luigi Caretto's store features classic examples of traditional Piedmontese interior design and includes period furniture, art deco lamps, and eighteenth-century art. The store feels as much of a museum as the nearby galleries at the Accorsi Foundation.

MARCO CAPPELLO
via Piazza Palazzo di Città, 21/b · ☎ 011.436.1245

Modern antiques including ceramics by the under-appreciated Italian designer Antonia Campi, late-1960s furniture by Anon, and a selection of unusual lighting like a 1970s lamp by Gino Valle. Cappello's roomy shop exemplifies a renewed interest here in avant-garde Italian design.

REGGIO AND MILANESE ANTICHITÀ RESTAURO
via Giolitti, 40/e, f, g · ☎ 011.835.147

Gabriele Reggio and his partner share three shopfronts between their antique wood restoration business and the shop that sells the results of their efforts. The store has the atmosphere of a workshop and is nurtured by people who care about the history behind the pieces they sell. An ever-changing stock includes eighteenth-century mirrors, nineteenth-century chairs, mid-twentieth-century chandeliers, and even early twentieth-century wood hat forms that I've been collecting from them for years.

13 PORTA PALATINA
via Porta Palatina, 13 · ☎ 011.347.730.4095

Mariola Demaglio and Giancarlo Cristiani's store is just a short walk from Piazza Repubblica and the Quadrilatero. You can leave their carefully curated shop with anything from mid-century furniture or African sculpture to more easily transportable vintage Balenciaga jewelery.

FOOD & WINE

THE CENTER OF TURIN IS RELATIVELY FREE OF LARGE SUPERMARKETS; THE TORINESI still tend to shop daily for their groceries at outdoor markets and specialty shops, and the individuality and reliability of the market vendors and shopkeepers scattered throughout the city are a testament to the quality local food-lovers expect and demand. Championed by the Slow Food movement, based in nearby Bra, the regional cooking of Piedmont is based on local produce, seasonally prepared.

Outdoor markets are a vital source and laboratory of local ingredients throughout the year. The giant market at Piazza della Repubblica is worth visiting to experience its vast size and sheer dynamism. Porta Palazzo, as it is commonly called, is the largest outdoor market in Europe, and sells not only fresh food, but kitchen utensils, cheap shoes, and knock-off handbags. Don't be dissuaded by the crowds or the decidedly ungastronomical nature of some of the vendors—Porta Palazzo is energetic, enjoyably chaotic, and a unique experience in Turin. In the spring and summer, the market overflows with stalls selling cherries from Cuneo, asparagus of all shades, peaches from Canale, baby fennel; in the autumn, tables are fragrant carpets of mushrooms and artichokes. Locally-reared, and often organic, meat is standard fare; selling anything but Piedmontese dairy products is almost unheard of.

But, in general, I prefer the smaller, more manageable market at Piazza Madama Cristina (near the synagogue, and bordering the burgeoning multiethnic San Salvario neighborhood) and the Crocetta market (also popular for its numerous stalls of cut-price fashions). In addition, there are monthly *oasi dei prodotti tipici*—regular monthly markets specializing in local products—held at Piazza Palazzo di Città (first Sunday) and at Piazza Madama Cristina (third Sunday). The pleasure of these markets, in particular, is having the chance to see and speak with growers and producers in a calmer environment than the bustle of the daily markets. It's not uncommon to meet farmers wearing feathered alpine hats (sometimes bearing the badges of the Resistance brigades they fought in during the Second World War) and speaking Piedmontese (which sounds like the cross between French and Italian that it is) with each other. Finally, occasional organic-only markets are held at various venues and showcase vegetables, locally-produced honeys, confections, homemade grappas, and much more. Posters for these markets are displayed at the regular markets.

Wine shops often double as *enoteche*, where you can enjoy a drink from the offerings of nearby vineyards. Until recently, it was difficult to find non-Italian (and even non-Piedmontese) wine in all but the finest wine shops. This is beginning to change as a number of shops carve out small niches for themselves (regional Italian, Australian, or French wine, and even whiskies and spirits from abroad). It goes without saying that being in Turin is reason enough to sample the enormous variety of wine from Piedmont (especially simpler reds such as Barbera, Dolcetto, and Nebbiolo, and whites such as Roero) and to indulge in small tastings to discover what you really enjoy.

Gorgonzola—of which there are seven DOP varieties and even more imitators—may be the most characteristic cheese of the region, but two other southern Piedmontese cheeses, Toma and Robiola, are likely to be on every cheese cart in the restaurants, and you might find dozens of varieties of the former in the *formaggerie* around town. While produced throughout Piedmont, many of the best Tomas come from Cuneo and are made from semi-cooked cow's milk. Robiola, made with either sheep, cow, or goat milk, is typically produced around Asti and Alessandria (and has been since the Middle Ages). Other local cheeses to keep an eye out for are Paglierina, at its ripe best when oozing from the rind; the semi-hard Castelmagno; and the young sheep's milk Murazzano.

Turin is without argument the European home of chocolate. Introduced to Italy from Spain when Carlo Emanuele I married Princess Caterina, it was once only a royal indulgence. In 1678 the Savoys entrusted Giovambattista Ari with manufacturing a drinkable version for sale to the public. The first mass-produced chocolate was made by the Caffarel company in 1826, but it wasn't until forty years later that the same company created what has become Turin's trademark confection, *gianduiotto*—a rich, wedge-shaped chocolate and hazelnut candy, first made for the 1867 carnival and named after Gianduja, the *commedia dell'arte* character. Today local shops and producers, many of them in their original nineteenth-century locations, proudly show off endless chocolate creations. Easter and Christmas are especially good times not just to shop for unusual styles, but also to see beautiful window displays at the chocolatiers.

It is worth noting what may seem the eccentric opening hours many food and wine shops in Turin (as in much of Italy) keep. Butchers and breadshops, for example, are typically shut on Wednesday afternoons (as are many of the local supermarkets), and almost all shops in the city are closed for the languorous lunch hours of 12:30 to 3:00 pm.

Finally, the biannual Salone del Gusto, hosted by Slow Food, takes over the Lingotto Fiere for a week every other October (even years only). It emphasizes regional food from all over the world, but stalls and events hosted by Italian growers and producers stand out. Tastings, lectures, and food- and wine-oriented events keep thousands of visitors well-fed, well-informed, and entertained.

MARKETS

CROCETTA MARKET
Largo Cassini
Hours: 7:30–1 Mon–Fri; 7:30–5 Sat

MADAMA CRISTINA MARKET
Piazza Madama Cristina
Hours: 8–2 Mon–Sat

OASI DEI PRODOTTI TIPICI
Piazza Palazzo di Città
Hours: 9–6 first Sun of every month
& Piazza Madama Cristina
Hours: 9–6 third Sun of every month

PORTA PALAZZO MARKET
Piazza della Reppublica
Hours: 7:30–1 Mon–Fri; 7:30–7:30 Sat

CHEESE

BAITA DEL FORMAGG
via Lagrange, 36 · ☎ *011.562.3224*
The playful sign at Pierluigi Castagno's shop underplays
its sophisticated stock of cheeses from Piedmont and neighboring regions of France. Dozens of varieties vie for space
in the window display and range from a modest, farmhouse
Toma to a €30/kilo Castelmagno.

BERA BRUNA
via San Tommaso, 13 · ☎ *011.547.653*
Once the busiest *latteria* in the city, supplying milk and
cheese to homes and restaurants, Bera Bruna still sells some

of the finest *panna montata* and Piedmontese cheeses in Turin. The store's mid-century decor is almost untouched since its opening, and the wonderfully warm women staffing the store are as happy to talk about Turin's history as about its cheese.

BORGIATTINO FORMAGGI
via Cernaia, 32 · ☎ 011.535.237

ROBERTO BORGIATTINO
via della Accademia Albertina, 38/a · ☎ 011.839.4686

Established in 1927 on via Cernaia, Borgiattino Formaggi carries one of the finest and most diverse selection of Piedmontese cheeses (along with a small selection of imported ones). I prefer Roberto's shop on Accademia Albertina for its proximity to the market at Madama Cristina and for its proprietor's boundless enthusiasm and helpfulness; it seems more like a locally-frequented shop than a museum to cheese. It also carries a small selection of wines and meats.

WINE

ANTICA ENOTECA DEL BORGO
via Monferrato, 4 · ☎ 011.819.0461

A lovely wine shop near Gran Madre that stocks a wide array of Piedmontese wines, as well as—unusual for Turin—a selection of wines from Australia and California. On the charming via Monferrato, Marco and Federica Peyron's shop also doubles as a wine bar where neighborhood locals can enjoy an *aperitivo* before heading up the street to Monferrato for dinner.

CASA DEL BAROLO
via Andrea Doria, 7 · ☎ 011.532.038

The two-floor Casa del Barolo is an upmarket shop selling some of the finest Piedmontese labels available to a clientele that knows its wine. Perhaps not the place to purchase your everyday drinking wine, its elegant presentation says gift shop more than local wine shop. However, the selection is an education in itself and the staff always welcomes browsers.

LA CAVE À MILLÉSIMES
Corso De Gasperi, 21 · ☎ 011.593.112

A bright shop that specializes somewhat in fine French labels, but features the best Italian varieties in addition to wines from some unusual, small producers and a good selection of spirits and liqueurs from Italy and abroad. The staff is warm, knowledgeable, and ready to answer questions.

LA PETITE CAVE
Corso De Gasperi, 2/b · ☎ 011.595.208

A counter, a few tables, and warm service complement a range of mainly Italian labels in this wee, but excellent *enoteca*. At aperitif time, order a glass of wine and the owners will bring you a plate of the finest local *salumi* and cheese to accompany your tipple.

MILLE VIGNE
via Botero, 7/a · ☎ 011.381.9637

The lovely brick-vaulted room upstairs at Mille Vigne contains reasonably priced, quality Piedmontese wine (everything is under €10); pricier vintages are kept in a downstairs cellar. This Quadrilatero shop makes for good browsing or an easy place to pick up some well-priced everyday bottles.

PAROLA
Corso Vittorio Emanuele II, 76   011.650.2183
& via Cesare Battisti, 7 · ☎ 011.517.4162

The Vittorio Emanuele shop opened in 1890 and not much seems to have changed since then. Under the vaulted, painted ceilings, dusty vintages line the tops of wooden cases along the walls that hold regional wines and spirits. The sprightly Cesare Battisti store, much more recently opened, boasts an equally good, if more international, selection, and becomes an *enoteca* at aperitif time.

TABERNA LIBRERIA
via Bogino, 5 · ☎ 011.836.515

In the shadow of the Biblioteca Nazionale's hulking addition and a block from via Po, the combination of books and wine at Taberna Libreria works beautifully. Half the shop is dedicated to the finest Piedmontese labels (and some others) and a counter where one can enjoy *aperitivi* among local wine afficionados. The other side of the shop offers a wide selection of books related to wine and gastronomy: wine guides, cookbooks, nearly the entire Slow Food catalog, and a selection of regional food products ranging from sweets to spices to local honeys and preserves.

VINI RENATO RABEZZANA
via San Francesco d'Assisi, 23/c · ☎ *011.543.070*
Established in Turin in 1913 and presided over by Carlo Rabezzana (the founder's grandson), this petite shop (and downstairs cellar) sells the family's organically produced wine from San Desiderio di Calliano d'Asti, along with all the finest Piedmontese labels, plus some foreign spirits. They prepare custom gift boxes, of which there is a wide variety available, especially around the holidays. They also ship.

CHOCOLATE AND CONFECTIONS

CONFETTERIA AJIORDANO
Piazza Carlo Felice, 69 · ☎ *011.547.121*
Since 1857, Ajiordano's classic storefront and pleasingly cramped interior—with its walnut countertops, silvered mirrors, and antique jars—has displayed only Piedmontese confections. The proprietor, Rosalba Massimi, inherited the store from her aunt, who worked for the original owners, the Giordano family, for fifty years. Giftboxes of artisanal

gianduiotti are available.

CREMERIA GHIGO
via Po, 52 · ☎ 011.887.017

If the art deco chrome shopfront and cafe counter don't draw you in, then the confections on display—*marrons glacés*, tubs of *panna montata*, and, at Christmas time, freshly made *pan d'oro*—will. Ghigo, in the most pleasant way, looks and feels caught in another time. The hot chocolate in winter should not be missed, nor should their summer gelato window. Standing at the counter with a *cafè* and watching locals buy their sweets is entertaining, too.

GUIDO GOBINO
via Cagliari, 15/b · ☎ 011.247.6245

Off the beaten path from the Centro (a short ride on the number 27 bus from via Rossini, near the Mole; alight at the first stop on the other side of the Dora), this small shop is worth the effort to find. The white, modern interior is unlike any other in Turin: a kind of futuristic laboratory of chocolate. The excellent—if not wholly traditional—artisanal products are delicious and elegantly packaged. Their original miniature *gianduiotti*, called *turinot*, are extremely popular, but the extra bitter chocolate with traces of lemon or cinnamon, sold in *cubi*, may be my favorite.

PASTICCERIA GERLA
Corso Vittorio Emanuele II, 88 · ☎ 011.545.422

Gerla's original wooden shopfront and interior are a step back in time. Like so many other choclatiers in Turin, every product in this chocolate workshop is of high quality, including the pralines and the not-always-available gelato—when it is, try the chocolate, of course.

PASTICCERIA GERTOSIO
via Lagrange, 24/h · ☎ 011.562.1942

In the same spot since 1880 and family-run to this day, homemade chocolates and cakes are the specialty here. Try the hot chocolate at the bar or any of the forty-six flavors of pralines.

PEYRANO
Corso Vittorio Emanuele II, 76 · ☎ 011.538.765
& via Andrea Doria, 4/bis · ☎ 011.517.1641
& Corso Moncalieri, 47 · ☎ 011.660.2202

One of the oldest names in chocolate production in Turin, having been founded here in 1915, Peyrano now has three shops and has opened new ones in Rome and Naples. Chocolates may be bought at the shop attached to the kitchens and laboratory in Corso Moncalieri; pastries and exquisite, artistic chocolates at the Vittorio Emanuele shop (called Peyrano-Pfatish, as it was owned until 1963 by the Pfatish family, see below); and elegantly packaged giftboxes at the Andrea Doria boutique.

PFATISH
via Sacchi, 42 · ☎ 011.568.3962

Owned by a member of the Ferraris chocolate family, Pfatish is perhaps the most recognizable name in confections in Turin. Gustavo Pfatish, an Austrian, brought his original sweets and cakes to Turin in the mid-nineteenth century, amplifying the city's love affair with chocolate. At the via Sacchi shop, marble counters and wooden cases are piled high with pralines, cakes, and, of course, *gianduiotti*.

OTHER

BAUDRACCO
Corso Vittorio Emanuele II, 62 · ☎ 011.545.582

Baudracco covers all gastronomic needs: confections and cakes, an assortment of savory dry goods and oils, mouth-watering prepared food, and a selection of international cheeses. A lovely old store under the porticoes along Vittorio Emanuele that makes a good neighbor to the other culinary delights on this block.

BERA
via San Tommaso, 12 · ☎ 011.542.663

The effusive Marta Bera, whose sister runs the *latteria* across the street, has made excellent focaccia, *grissini*, and traditional everyday breads since 1969 and sells them in her Quadrilatero shop along with traditional sweet biscuits and cookies—all made by her. She also carries a selection of dry goods such as jams, honeys, and sauces.

P.A.I.S.S.A.

Piazza San Carlo, 196 · ☎ 011.562.8462

Infamously indifferent service may be what now character-
izes this classic shop under the porticoes of Piazza San Carlo,
but at one time it was the only food importer in Turin. More
a curiosity shop than grocery store, expats (and curious Italians) can now buy anything from Marmite to Oreos to a
variety of Italian specialty foods. Still loved, they carry an
impressive selection of Piedmontese wines and spirits. The
name is an acronym for *Prodotti Alimentari Italiani e Stra-
nieri Società Anonima.*

PASTIFICIO DEFILIPPIS

via Lagrange, 39 · ☎ 011.542.137

My husband and I used to live around the corner from
Defilippis, and it was a rare day that we left the store
without a ribbon-tied parcel of *agnolotti* or *tagliatelle "per
due,"* sometimes with a complementary handful of sage
from Angela. This is probably the best pasta shop in the
city, if not for choice—they make eight or nine varieties
fresh daily in the back kitchen in addition to a selection
of prepared foods and dry pasta—then for atmosphere.
A turn-of-the-last-century wooden and glass shopfront,
friendly service, cooking advice, and careful packaging
make Defilippis one of the most pleasant places to shop for
provisions in the city.

STEFFANONE
via Maria Vittoria, 2 · ☎ 011.546.737

The prepared foods and cold meats at Steffanone are some of the finest—and priciest—in the city. The knowledgable, white-smocked and hatted owners sell only the best quality local hams and a small selection of cheeses. They also have dry goods, a fine wine selection, and make a homemade *finanziera* to take home.

WALTER FICINI
via Berthollet, 30 · ☎ 011.669.9558

The wonderful Madama Cristina market is itself surrounded by some of the best food buying to be had in Turin. Quite apart from the fine local produce and meat at the market itself, one can stock up on cheeses, fresh pasta, and, at Ficini, some very fine bread. The endless choices—rye, fennel and anise, *grissini* (three or four types!), spelt—are not limited to strictly Italian-style loaves. There is also a wide choice of focaccia and pizza to take away by the slice.

KIDS

✹

THERE'S PLENTY IN TURIN TO KEEP CHILDREN OCCUPIED AND STIMULATED. One of the most appealing aspects of many of the city's civic and cultural attractions is their universal age appeal; it's not uncommon to see large school groups of under-tens being toured around the dense Museo del Risorgimento or the former royal palaces. Perhaps some of the best days out for kids, however, would involve a clattering ride on one of the city's few remaining old orange trams (numbers 13 and 16 are good choices, cutting right through the heart of the city), a visit to the Museo Egizio's relics (coupled with a gelato at nearby Pepino, of course) to decipher the hieroglyphs and then onto the Museo di Zoologia's great ribcage-shaped hall of animals. You could do worse than ending a long day with a pizza at Pizzeria Alla Baita dei Sette Nani or Spaccanapoli.

The one-car railway up to Superga, its adjacent wooded park with room to run and roam make a nice, long outing; dramatic views of the mountains on a sunny day would amaze any child and the creepy, cold vaults in the Savoy mausoleum are decorated with plenty of coats-of-arms, gargoyles, and other sinister statuary to keep children amused while the tour guide drones on about the former royalty interred within.

The most astonishing destination for any kid or adult, however, may be the Museo Nazionale del Cinema. Make your way up the ramp, through the camera obscura and zoetropes, watch old movies, see Italian posters of your favorite films, then take the "panoramic lift" to the observation deck, marvel at the view across the city and out to the Alps, and pick out the rooftops and bell towers of the buildings you've visited and follow the trams clamoring across the bridge, where in the summer months, an open-air, interactive museum called Experimenta appears in the Parco Michelotti (call 800 329 329 for detailed information on opening dates and times).

Turin is blessed with some lovely outdoor spaces when tykes just need to run. The Parco del Valentino (with the adjacent Borgo Medioevale) and the grounds at Stupinigi are well-suited to half-day trips, with acres and acres of green and wooded areas to explore; while the city's green piazzas, including Piazza Cavour and dog-filled Piazza Maria Teresa are well-placed for short breaks on longer walks between sights and *gelati*.

A walking tour of chocolate shops doesn't need to

be limited to children, but they will no doubt marvel at the variety of sweets available and enjoy the attention and free samples from shopkeepers. Walking along the north side of Corso Vittorio Emanuele II under the arcades reveals Peyrano, Ajiordano, and Gerla—a virtually endless stream of chocolate, sugar, cakes, and grand window displays in nineteenth- and early twentieth-century storefronts adults can appreciate as much as the confections within.

HOTELS

There is no shortage of hotels in Turin, but they have traditionally catered to business travellers, and the bland decor and indifferent service of the typical business hotel predominates. Still, there are a number of smaller, privately run hotels throughout the city. Most higher-end hotels in Turin are managed by the chains—Best Western and Jolly prevail—and almost all hotels below a three-star rating are quite basic and drab. The quality even among three-star hotels can vary from spartan post-war design to up-to-the-minute modern comfort.

The list below focuses on the best three-star family-owned options. Most of these hotels are in the heart of the city, close to museums, restaurants, and cafes, and all are reasonably convenient to public transport. Since choosing a B&B is very much a matter of personal taste I list only two. In addition, there is the option of organizing *agriturismo* in the city environs—if you choose this route, check *www.agriturismoitalia.com* for guidance.

The Torinesi (indeed the Italians, generally) don't eat much in the way of breakfast so you may be disappointed with what's on offer if a morning meal is included in your stay. Unless you choose a B&B, I would recommend foregoing breakfast options at the hotels and seeking out the nearest neighborhood cafe for your morning coffee and

175

brioche. You'll get to know the barista, who will almost invariably greet you with a hearty *Buon giorno!* every morning (I guarantee they'll remember the way you take your coffee, too), and the activity around the bar is much more rewarding than cold eggs and dry toast in a hotel's breakfast room.

A B +
via Porta Palatina, 23/b · ☎ *011.433.8732*
www.progettocluster.com
★★★★

Three sumptiously remodelled apartments available for rent above the restaurant of the same name in one of the oldest houses in Turin. AB+ (pronounced "ah-bee-pyoo") is a short walk from the market at Porta Palazzo, a bevy of restaurants and museums, and the Quadrilatero district, and makes for an interesting, but expensive self-catering option. Mid-century modern furniture and sleek kitchens fit in surprisingly well with the restored tile floors and ancient stuccoed walls.

AMADEUS E TEATRO
via Principe Amedeo, 41/b ☎ *011.817.4951*
www.turinhotelcompany.com
★★★

With an excellent location near the via Po and the lively Spada Reale restaurant, the twenty-four room Amadeus e Teatro may not be much to look at from the outside, but has better than serviceable rooms and is surprisingly quiet. The university is quite near, lending to the youthful and arty atmosphere of the neighborhood, and many of Turin's historic cafes are within a few minutes walk. Rates are on the higher end of the three-star scale.

CASA MARGA
via Bava, 1 bis · ☎ 011.883.892
No website; e-mail: casamarga@hotmail.com
Bed and Breakfast

Near Piazza Vittorio Veneto and the river, Margarita Corongiu lets out two rooms—both with private baths—in her own home at remarkably reasonable prices. Margarita's breakfasts, including her homemade jams, are recommended.

GRAND HOTEL SITEA
via Carlo Alberto, 35 · ☎ 011.517.0171
www.sitea.thi.it
★★★★

Located in the Centro, the elegant and discreet Sitea also boasts a fine restaurant, the Carignano. Often host to visiting footballers, actors, and politicians, the hotel has four-star prices to suit its famous clientele.

HOTEL BOSTON
via Massena, 70 · ☎ 011.500.359
www.hotelbostontorino.it
★★★★

Perhaps the most unusual hotel in the city, the Hotel Boston is filled with contemporary art—paintings by Lucio Fontana, Carla Accardi, and Giuseppe Penone, for example—and antique rugs. Located in the Crocetta neighborhood, it is beyond easy walking distance of most of Turin's cultural attractions (except the GAM), but it does offer a quiet option in a lovely residential neighborhood, which also features the bustling Crocetta market six days a week. Getting into the Centro is a matter of a ten minute bus or tram ride. Not to everyone's taste, the Boston nonetheless offers friendly service and large, quiet rooms at rates well below some choices in the Centro. Also available is an ultra-modern penthouse loft for longer stays.

HOTEL CONTE BIANCAMANO
Corso Vittorio Emanuele II, 73 · ☎ 011.562.3281
www.hotelcontebiancamano.it
★★★

Located on the third floor of a nineteenth-century palazzo, the hotel's twenty-four rooms are less grand than the chandeliered and stuccoed public areas might suggest. However, they are soundproofed against traffic noise, and Laura and Roberto Ravella's cozy, family-run hotel is a good, intimate choice in the Centro, at perfectly reasonable rates.

HOTEL DOGANA VECCHIA

via Corte d'Appello, 4 · ☎ *011.436.6752*
www.hoteldoganavecchia.com
★★★

The welcoming staff at the Dogana Vecchia is only one of its qualities: it's in an eighteenth-century building; it's just steps from the heart of the Quadrilatero; many of its fifty rooms are furnished with antiques (others are austere compared to the elegant lobby, so you may want to request one of the more characteristic rooms); and the rates are, surprisingly, given its excellent location, at the lower end of three stars.

HOTEL SOLFERINO & ARTUA

via Brofferio, 1 · ☎ *011.517.5301*
www.artua.it
★★★

Actually two hotels side-by-side, owned by the Vottero family. On a small side street near the Piazza Solferino, the fourth floors of two adjoining *palazzi* have been turned into private ten-room hotels. The Artua has an elegant wood and glass elevator to its lobby, and both hotels enjoy the privacy and quiet of a short, residential street.

LE MERIDIEN LINGOTTO
via Nizza, 262 · ☎ 011.664.2000
★★★★

LE MERIDIEN ART+TECH
via Nizza, 230 · ☎ 011.664.2000
www.lemeridien-lingotto.it
★★★★★

Both Le Meridien hotels have been thoughtfully and dramatically designed by Renzo Piano and are situated within the former FIAT factory at Lingotto, at the southern edge of the city; they're most convenient if you are visiting in conjunction with an event at the Lingotto conference center. Between the distance from the Centro (a twenty-plus minute bus ride) and the very high rates for rooms, Le Meridien may not seem like an appealing choice except for the most design-conscious, but the view of the Alps from the test track on top of the building and the proximity to a cinema, the Pinacoteca Giovanni e Marella Agnelli, and a lush courtyard garden may be enough to lure you.

LIBERTY
via Pietro Micca, 15 · ☎ 011.562.8801
www.hotelliberty-torino.it
★★★

Liberty, as its name suggests, is on the top floor of an art nouveau building steps from the Quadrilatero. Wood floors, old rugs, period beds, and a great location made the Liberty popular with visiting writers and artists decades ago.

SAVOIA

via del Carmine, 1/b · ☎ 011.339.125.7711
www.infinito.it/utenti/aisavoia/
Bed and Breakfast

A reliable B&B located in the former apartments of the Palazzo Saluzzo Paesana, an early eighteenth-century palace and one of the largest in the city. The courtyard has a stunning double-height *loggia*. Rooms have eighteenth-century decorations and nineteenth-century furniture, and rates, although higher than most B&Bs, are very good for the quality of the rooms.

VICTORIA

via Nino Costa, 4 · ☎ 011.561.1909
www.hotelvictoria-torino.com
★★★

Located in a nondescript building on a small pedestrianized street equidistant from Piazza Carlina and the Museo Egizio, the Victoria is somewhat overdecorated in the English country style. But it is popular, more comfortable than its facade implies, and rather intimate for a 100-room hotel. The lobby and public rooms on the ground floor are welcoming, as is the staff. Weekend rates are attractive given the location and quality of the hotel.

EXCURSIONS NEAR AND FAR

❦

LA COLLINA AND BORGO PO

Some of Turin's most evocative views and experiences lie in the neighborhoods and villages in the surrounding hills. The fresh air, space, and wilderness drew wealthy nobles there in the fifteenth and sixteenth centuries and the Savoys built hillside retreats there, called *vigne*. By the end of the sixteenth century, so many families had invaded the hills that writer Giovanni Botero wrote that the villages of La Collina could "constitute a second Turin." By the end of the eighteenth century, the variety of *vigne*, hunting lodges, parks, and gardens dotted among the woodlands was diverse enough to call for a guide to their styles and owners, written by Amedeo Grossi, in 1790. The prestige associated with the *vigne* was measurable, and it became *de rigeur* to build farther and farther away from the center, as it displayed the wealth and resources needed to do so. As the Savoy families died off or were exiled, the hills closer to the city became less exclusive, if still associated with a more affluent class. In the twentieth century, larger apartment blocks were built side-by-side with art noveau homes, and distinctive neighborhoods began to form.

City planning efforts in the mid-1950s, called for strategies to better connect the city to the hills, but visions of funiculars, wide boulevards, and tourist-friendly hotels and restaurants in the area went unrealized (perhaps thankfully). Today, quiet, isolated residential areas pepper the slopes, and examples of fantastic—in some cases, fantastically decaying—Liberty and eclectic architecture sit tucked away, underappreciated. Despite the planning failure many of the neighborhoods are reachable by public transit from Piazza Vittorio Veneto, by car, or better yet, on foot, at least for the nearer ones, like the Borgo Po just across the Ponte Vittorio Emanuele II. (Sometimes referred to as the "stone bridge," it was built under Napoleon, in 1814, and makes a natural starting point for a trip into the hills.)

Every few weekends, an antiques market appears in Piazza Gran Madre di Dio, offering large pieces of restored period furniture, great vintage Italian clothing and hats, and magazines and posters from the early 1900s. The church, designed after the Pantheon by Fernando Buonsignore (who worked in Turin for the French government, who in turn rejected many of his designs and destroyed what they did commission from him), was completed in 1831, on the return of the Savoys from exile. In addition to some statuary typical of the time by Bruneri, Finelli, and Rubino, it contains an ossuary which holds the remains of 5,000 Piedmontese who died during World Wars I and II. The church is built upon a base in order to improve the view of it from a distance along via Po. The piazza around the church was intended to be as rigorous and architecturally harmonious as Piazza Vittorio Veneto, but the work was never fully carried out.

In the neighborhood, via Monferrato makes a useful centerpoint for an afternoon's visit. A lunch at Monferrato, a glass of wine at Antica enoteca del borgo, or a gelato in the piazza would be good bookends to an exploration of the neighborhood.

Beyond the church, the gentle slope of the hills begins. Straight ahead is Villa della Regina—a summer hamlet of the nobles. Designed by Vitozzi, and built beginning in 1618, it initially belonged to Cardinal Maurizio of Savoy, and was augmented over the years, notably by Amedeo di Castellamonte and, in the 1720s, by Juvarra, who probably planned the center garden. Badly damaged during World War II, it has been in a constant state of restoration ever since. It is now a UNESCO World Heritage site and due to reopen as a museum. A spectacular double staircase, flanked by terraced gardens and grottoes, leads to the main building, its double loggia topped by statues, hinting at the double-height, frescoed salon inside.

To the right sits the Monte dei Cappuccini; until the fifteenth century, its strategic site held a fort, complete with towers and battlements that controlled the bridge below. In 1583, Carlo Emanuele bought the land and donated it to the Capuchin order, for whom Vitozzi built a church and monastery—now the Church of Santa Maria al Monte—beautiful in its simplicity (though the simple drum roof replaced an elegant dome) and a distinctive landmark on the hillside skyline. Inside is a lovely altar designed by Carlo di Castellamonte and Alfieri, statuary by Clemente, and paintings by Cerano. Beside that is the Museo Nazionale della Montagna and a wonderful, panoramic view of the mountains: the steep hike is worth it.

CHIERI

A visit to the hilltop town of Chieri (accessible by the number 30 bus), about thirty minutes from the city, is a pleasant diversion. In Roman times the town was called *Karreo Potentiai* and later Cherium. Its winding cobbled streets probably resembled ancient Turin in layout, and it was one of the few inhabited villages in Piedmont at the time. It was home to the University of Turin from 1427–1434, just as the town became part of the Savoy kingdom. The churches of San Giorgio and San Domenico (site of the Turinese Athenaeum, where scholars and artists met and gave public talks), and the Piedmontese Gothic facade of the fifteenth-century Duomo—and the medieval houses and streets around them—are alone worth a visit. Chieri's past is intrinsically linked to Italy's textile industry, and its cotton, silk, and weaving trades were as active as those in parts of Flemish Belgium during the Middle Ages. The Museo del Tessile is dedicated to this history and can be visited by appointment. Though not readily accessible, the Osservatorio Meteorologico Real Collegio Carlo Alberto exhibits antique weather instruments and other scientific apparatus in booklined rooms. Call in advance to see if the Osservatorio is holding an open day or special exhibit (011.641.570). A good lunch option is San Domenico, at via San Domenico, 2/b (011.941.1864). La Cantina del Convento at vicolo Sant'Antonio, 6, is a good place for a glass of wine and *aperitivi* before heading back to Turin.

IVREA

North of Turin is the beautiful Valle d'Aosta, Ivrea is its gateway. The medieval town center has an unusual brick cathedral and is pleasant to walk around, unless you visit during the pre-Lenten Carnival, which brings out the crowds. On Ash Wednesday, in the Borghetto, you can join the residents in their traditional holiday meal of baccalà and polenta, if you do visit during Carnival.

Despite its peaceful valley setting and medieval surrounds, Ivrea boasts quite an industrial past. The Olivetti company, known for its sleek Lettera 22 typewriter (among other classics of modern product design), was founded here by Camilio Olivetti in 1907. The first typewriter he produced, the M1, was unveiled to the public at the 1911 Expo in Turin, and was famously advertised with a haunting image of Dante lording over one of the machines. Olivetti, and his son, Adriano, who took over operation of the firm in 1938, were pioneers of socially-conscious work policies and philanthropy. They introduced shorter working hours (with no reduction in pay), employee health care, housing for factory workers, nurseries for their children, and an environment designed by some of the most inventive architects of the day. While still based in Ivrea, Olivetti has become better known today for its copiers, printers, and, familiar to all Italians, its postal machines. In the same spirit that drove the creation of its innovative factories and workers' housing, the Olivetti complex has become something of an open air museum—the Museo a Cielo Aperto dell'Archittetura Moderna di Ivrea, or MAAM. You can take a self-guided tour of the buildings that constituted Olivetti's headquarters along via Jervis by picking up a map at the Cooperativa Contraverde at via Jervis, 77 (the way is also well marked with signs and explanatory texts). Alternatively, you can arrange a guided tour by calling in advance on 0125.43.206. Notable buildings include an early factory building from 1896, when Olivetti was still a small family concern, the nearby glass offices of the late 1950s, the Hotel la Serra housing estate, and the semi-circular Unità Residenziale Ovest. Trains leave Porta Nuova hourly, at least, and take about forty minutes. For architecture enthusiasts, a trip to Ivrea is highly recommended.

THE LANGHE AND MONFERRATO

Entire books are dedicated to the Langhe and Monferrato wine-making towns of southern Piedmont, but if you are planning a slightly longer trip to the region Asti, Alba, and nearby Bra make wonderful (if long-ish) days out of town, if you can't dedicate an entire weekend. In some cases, a car may be easier than relying on infrequent trains and local bus service (in the cases of Alba and Bra). Trains from Porta Nuova to Asti are frequent, and the journey under thirty minutes. To Alba, the trains are hourly (and via Asti). Bra is the home of Slow Food and the organization's excellent *Itinerari Slow* books on the area should be your guides.

SKIING

Turin's existing infrastructure for skiing, west of the city, near the French border, was the key to its successful bid to host the 2006 winter Olympic games. The season here runs November through April and the resorts are within easy reach of the city by train, car, and bus. In the Val di Susa, the largest resort is at Bardonecchia, on the French border, with thirty lifts and 150km of slopes. In the Val Chisone a group of neighboring pistes called the Via Lattera (Milky Way) is extremely popular and includes renowned spots Sestrière and Clavière, from which the French slopes of Montegenèvre can be reached. Winter trekking, ice skating, and snowshoeing are available at nearly all the resorts and are good options for non-skiers who would still like to enjoy the majesty of the Italian Alps. More detailed information on the resorts is available at *www.vialattea.it* and *www. montagnedoc.it.*

ESSENTIALS

TRANSIT

Getting into the city center from the airport is pretty straightforward. I do not recommend taking a taxi, it can be well over €30 one way and the queue can be interminable. The blue and yellow Sadem bus into the Centro is reliable and comfortable, can be boarded right outside the arrivals terminal every thirty to forty-five minutes, and leaves you at Porta Nuova after a forty minute journey. (Sadem, ☎ 011.300.0611, €5. Tickets can be purchased from automated machines in the terminal; a €0.50 surcharge applies to tickets purchased on board; discounts for Torino Card holders, see below).

An express train from the airport is available, but at the time of writing, it travels only as far as Dora Station, which is not particularly convenient for the Centro (but more so if you are staying in the Quadrilatero). It runs twice an hour, takes twenty minutes to reach Dora station, and your ticket will allow transfers to city buses and trams within a seventy minute period. The service will soon extend to the more central Porta Susa station. (GTT, ☎ 800.691.0000, €3. Tickets can be purchased from automated machines in the terminal).

If you are travelling to Turin on an international train, you're likely to disembark at Porta Susa, which is a good bus and tram transfer point for more central destinations. If you come into Porta Nuova there are endless bus and tram options to all points, and both stations have taxi ranks.

Turin's public transport system is efficient, well-used, and wide-reaching. For a €0.90 fare, you can get as far as the museum at Rivoli or the lovely medieval town of Chieri (both about eight miles away). Though walking in the city center is by far the easiest, most pleasant, and sometimes quickest option, it is well served by buses and trams. Unfortunately, the lovely clanking orange trams of yesteryear are being replaced by larger, quieter, and modern silver and blue trams, which have dedicated lanes on the road and are quicker than buses. By the time the Olympic games come to town a short section of the ambitious new subway system should be operating in the Centro.

If you do plan on using public transit, and I encourage it, the simplest ticket purchase is a *bloccato* of fifteen bus/ tram tickets at €12.50. Fares cannot be purchased from the driver, but can be bought at newsagents, *tabacchi*, and in some bars. Tickets must be validated in the orange machines on board and are good for any number of trips within seventy minutes from the time stamped. Children under a meter tall ride free, older children (or taller ones!) pay an adult fare.

There are other discounted fare options available. Depending on the length and nature of your trip, the best options are: *Giornalero*, which allows twenty-four hour unlimited travel at €3; the *Viaggiare insieme* allows up to four people travelling together unlimited rides between 2:30–8 pm on weekends only; and the *Settimanale Formula U*, which at €8.50, allows unlimited travel for a calendar week.

ATRIUM

This new structure, created by car designer Giorgetto Giugiaro and housed in Piazza Solferino, is aimed at making cultural and tourist information easily accessible to visitors and locals alike. The two parts of the building house AtriumCittà and Atrium2006. The former has an elaborate display about the history of the city and its future plans for development, which is worth browsing for the old film footage of Turin and the detailed maps and models outlining the city's ambitious plans. Atrium2006 has a helpful tourist desk, in addition to historical and current information about the winter Olympic games. ☎ 011.516.2006; open 9:30 am–7 pm every day.

TORINO CARD

TurismoTorino offers a tourist-friendly city card that allows free entry to most of the major museums in the city and includes free travel on city buses and trams; discounts at museum bookshops; and reduced-priced theater and concert tickets at selected venues. It can also be presented for free boarding of the Sassi-Superga railway, the panoramic lift at the Mole Antonelliana, and some riverboat services on the Po. It can be purchased at the Atrium, airport and Porta Nuova tourist desks, many hotels, and many of the larger participating museums. 48-hour card: €15; 72-hour card: €17.

TORINO SETTE

La Stampa's Friday supplement, *Torino Sette*, is essential if you're spending even a few days in the city. Its exhaustive listings distill the week's events at museums, clubs, theaters, and concert venues, as well as providing a summary of lectures, book readings, and events in the city and throughout Piedmont. It reviews restaurants, clubs, bars, and even gelato (in a weekly column called "Gelato Dream") and announces new store openings and special market days. One of its best and most unusual features is a two-page section written in, and devoted to, events in the Piedmontese dialect.

FURTHER READING
ABOUT TURIN

IT WAS ONLY IN THE NINETEENTH CENTURY THAT TURIN'S STATUS AS A LITERARY CENTER began to be recognized. Political writing came into its own during the Risorgimento, and the works of Mazzini, Cavour, and Garibaldi continue to be widely read throughout Italy and are still available in popular editions.

In 1933, Giulio Einaudi, son of Luigi Einaudi, the Italian Republic's first president, founded the Einaudi publishing house in Turin. An influential figure from the start, Giulio Einaudi published Antonio Gramsci, Italo Calvino (who also worked as an editor there), and Natalia Ginzburg—and was even jailed for his "subversive" acts of publishing.

With the rise of Fascism, important dissenting voices in twentieth-century literature and politics emerged from the experiences of living under the regime or as partisans during the war, and, in the case of Turin-born Primo Levi, from concentration camps. What follows is a list of books by key Torinese writers and other books inspired by the city.

ALESSANDRO BARICCO
Novocento and *City*

Turin-born Baricco doesn't write about Turin and now lives in Rome, but is perhaps the most celebrated young novelist to come out of the city in decades. He established the Holden School in Turin for young writers.

ITALO CALVINO
Marcovaldo, Invisible Cities and
The Path to the Nest of Spiders

Calvino, though not a Turin native, moved there after fighting in the Resistance as a young man. He wrote about his experience as a partisan in his first book, *The Path to the Nest of Spiders*; in the introduction to later editions he wrote that his work on the subject could never compare to that of Beppe Fenoglio. Later novels, and those for which he is justifiably most well-known, *Marcovaldo* and *Invisible Cities*, were both written in Turin.

LESLEY CHAMBERLAIN
Nietzsche in Turin: The End of the Future

An excellent account of Nietzsche's "miraculous" year in Turin and the atmosphere that surrounded some of his most significant work.

GIUSEPPE CULICCHIA
Torino è casa mia

Culicchia's book is a touching, humorous, sometimes caustic, but stunningly accurate look at "his" Turin.

EDMONDO D'AMICIS CUORE
The Heart of a Boy

MASSIMO D'AZEGLIO
I miei riccordi

XAVIER DE MAISTRE
A Nocturnal Expedition Around My Room

NATALIA GINZBURG
Family Sayings and *All Our Yesterdays*

JEAN GIONO
An Italian Journey
Poet and novelist Giono visited Turin, his father's hometown, in 1951 and recorded his journey there and around the rest of Italy in this book.

PIERO GOBETTI
On Liberal Revolution

GUIDO GOZZANO
The Colloquies

ANTONIO GRAMSCI
La nostra città futura: scritti torinesi (1911–1922)
Less well-known than the prison diaries, Gramschi's pre-prison writings cover not only his fervent efforts at organizing workers and establishing worker education in Turin, but also some cultural writings from the time he established the newspaper, *L'Ordine Nuovo.*

BEPPE FENOGLIO
Johnny the Partisan

**ISTITUTO PIEMONTESE PER LA STORIA
DELLA RESISTENZA E DELLA SOCIETÀ
CONTEMPORANEA**
Torino 1938-1945: una guida per la memoria
A thorough guide to the war and occupation in Turin.

PRIMO LEVI
The Monkey's Wrench and *The Periodic Table*
Turin native Primo Levi is probably best known for writing
about his experiences at Auschwitz (*If Not Now, When?* and
Moments of Reprieve), but many of his books draw from
life in Turin. The "Potassium" chapter in the "memoir"
The Periodic Table focusses on his studies under the racial
laws and the physics tutor who took Levi on as a student
despite them.

CARLO LEVI
Christ Stopped at Eboli
Levi was a Turin-born physician, painter, writer, and
founder of the anti-fascist movement Giustizia e Libertà, who was exiled to Lucania in the rural south for his
activism. *Christ Stopped at Eboli* is a fictionalized account
of his year there.

FRIEDRICH NIETZSCHE
Ecce Homo

CESARE PAVESE
The House on the Hill

RENZO ROSSOTTI
Curiosità e misteri di Torino

ABOUT THE AUTHOR

EUGENIA BELL is a freelance writer and book editor. She has written for *Interiors*, *Artforum*, *ID* and *Lingua Franca*, and has edited books for the Hermitage Museum in St. Petersburg, the V&A in London, the Albertina in Vienna, and the Neue Galerie in New York. Born in New York, her family is from Turin and she's visited the city for years. She lives in London.

ACKNOWLEDGEMENTS

I owe many thanks to Nadia Aguiar at the Little Book-room for her enthusiasm for this project from the start and her thoughtful comments throughout the writing and editing process. Thanks to Louise Fili and Todd Pasini for giving true and elegant expression to Turin in print, and to Mario Pereira, whose eagle-eyed copy-editing and comments improved the manuscript considerably. And finally, my endless, heartfelt gratitude goes to Matt, not in the least because his love for Turin may possibly exceed my own, but without whose comments, encouragement, companionship, and good cheer this would have been a lesser book.